2003

W9-DFF-757

The Reference Shelf™

The American Family

Edited by Karen Duda

The Reference Shelf
Volume 75 • Number 2

The H.W. Wilson Company
2003

The Reference Shelf

The books in this series contain reprints of articles, excerpts from books, addresses on current issues, and studies of social trends in the United States and other countries. There are six separately bound numbers in each volume, all of which are usually published in the same calendar year. Numbers one through five are each devoted to a single subject, providing background information and discussion from various points of view and concluding with a subject index and comprehensive bibliography that lists books, pamphlets, and abstracts of additional articles on the subject. The final number of each volume is a collection of recent speeches, and it contains a cumulative speaker index. Books in the series may be purchased individually or on subscription.

Library of Congress has cataloged this title as follows:

The American Family / edited by Karen Duda.
        p.cm.—(The reference shelf; v. 75, no. 2)
    Includes bibliographical references and index.
    ISBN 0-8242-1020-4
    1. Family—United States. I. Duda, Karen. II. Series.

HQ536.A54653 2003
306.85'0973—dc21

2003042269

Cover: *Family Portrait*, by Stephen Simpson (Taxi)

Visit H.W. Wilson's Web site: www.hwwilson.com

Printed in the United States of America

Contents

Preface

The catch phrase "family values" has been appropriated by American politicians and religious organizations, as well as progressive groups and gay and lesbian rights organizations. But what does the typical American family look like? A father who earns a living by working in an office or factory, a mother who stays home to raise the children, and kids who play with their friends in the neighborhood until dinnertime? While 50 years ago the nuclear family—mother, father, and 2.3 children—might have been held up as the norm, such a model falls far short of describing the multitude of variations on the family in the United States today. This book serves as a guide to the richness of family life in the United States at the dawn of the 21st century. As we shall see, today's America encompasses homes led by divorced and single parents, stepfamilies, interfaith and interracial marriages, gay partnerships, childless couples, and the traditional nuclear family, as well as many other domestic structures.

As demographics have shifted, the circumstances of America's families have also changed. With the increased incidence of divorce, many children are being raised by only one parent; the stigma against children born to unmarried couples is rapidly disappearing; and some children know only one parent. Remarriage produces stepfamilies, and it is no longer unusual for children to be raised by grandparents or extended family members if a parent is unable to care for them.

Since the 1970s, women have had greater career opportunities, but today professional women are still faced with tough choices, chief among them whether to continue working after the arrival of children or to stay at home to raise them. A tiny percentage of fathers stay at home to raise their children, but in most families the burden of childrearing still falls disproportionately on women. Medical science offers women more control over when and if they have children, so many women delay childbearing to establish careers, while others advocate having children early so as not to interrupt a career later.

The boom in reproductive technology has also made it possible for previously infertile individuals (both married and unmarried, both young and middle-aged) to have biological children by a variety of methods, even those as controversial as human cloning. Nevertheless, adoption (often from a foreign country) remains popular. In addition, gay couples and individuals have gained the right to raise children, becoming parents either through reproductive technology or adoption, which would have been unthinkable a generation ago.

At the same time, couples that are childless by choice are challenging the old assumption that every married couple wants to raise a family. Some committed couples—whether or not they have children—live together in stable, long-term relationships without any plans of marriage, and interracial and interfaith unions are no longer the taboos they once were. As the percentage of non-white racial groups in the United States continues to grow, alternative family structures have gained prominence as well. Americans continue to insist on the importance of the family unit, even though the nation's plurality has ensured that there are as many definitions of "family" as there are ethnic groups in the United States.

Even among nuclear families, life is vastly different from what was portrayed on *Leave It to Beaver* or *The Donna Reed Show*. Families today are busier than ever and pulled in all directions. Rather than sitting down together for a family dinner, parents may be working late and children may be playing on a Little League soccer team, learning Spanish, or taking piano lessons. Parents who work often struggle to balance spending time with their family and the demands of the job, while low-income families may find it a challenge just to survive. Violence against children, spouses, and domestic partners remains a critical issue, along with the struggle to set boundaries for children and the attempt to shield them from the rampant materialism of American society.

The first section of this book, "The Changing Family," chronicles the ways in which families in the United States have altered since the nuclear family was considered the norm. Section II, "The Collective Majority," highlights those groups considered "minorities" in the United States and explores the meaning and structure of the family for them as compared with the white "majority." "Marriage and Other Partnerships," the third section, deals with the various forms adult romantic relationships take today. The fourth section of the book, "Families in Crisis," addresses many of the chief concerns of today's families, which often reflect the greater problems of American society. "Planning Parenthood," the fifth section, touches on the different methods of having and raising children—as well as deciding whether to have them at all. The final section, "Nontraditional Families," includes articles about gay parents, single parents, interethnic marriage, and the place of the nuclear family in America today.

I would like to thank the periodicals that gave permission to reprint their articles in this book. Special thanks as well to Lynn Messina, editor in General Reference, for her friendship and invaluable assistance in preparing this volume. My gratitude also goes to Cliff Thompson for allowing me to take time from my other assignments to prepare this book. Finally, thank you to my co-workers in *Current Biography* and General Reference who have made coming to work a pleasant and intellectually stimulating experience.

Karen Duda
April 2003

I. The Changing Family

Editor's Introduction

The American family has changed drastically in the last 50 years; living arrangements deemed impermissible in the immediate postwar years are now the norm. Adoption, divorce, and remarriage shape families more than they did in the past, as do caregiving issues and the influence of the extended family. Furthermore, unions that once might have excited considerable resistance, such as interfaith marriages and gay partnerships, are becoming more commonplace. Section I, by addressing these issues, presents an overview of the varied circumstances faced by today's American family.

In "The Adoption Maze," Kim Clark and Nancy Shute relate how it has become more difficult to adopt a child in America. Although the number of couples interested in adopting has risen, these prospective parents have been discouraged by high-profile cases of failed adoption attempts involving children sold illegally to unsuspecting couples or broken promises between birth mothers and adoption agencies. Difficulties in adopting children within the United States have led many couples to brave potential frustrations with red tape and cultural differences to adopt children from countries such as Russia, China, South Korea, and Guatemala, where children might be in poor health due to a lack of prenatal care and neglect by orphanages. Clark and Shute provide some background for these circumstances, as well as the changing attitudes towards adoption, which was once held as a family secret but is today celebrated as an act of love and generosity.

In "The Reappearing Nuclear Family," David Blankenhorn comments on two reports on the status of the traditional nuclear family, consisting of a married couple and their biological or adoptive children living under the same roof. Using statistics from various studies, he shows that the trend towards family fragmentation (including divorce, remarriage, and single parenthood) has reversed itself slightly since the mid-1990s, a condition he attributes to alterations in welfare laws and changed attitudes towards the importance of the nuclear family.

Roberta Israeloff explores the flipside of the traditional family structure in "Step by Step." Israeloff looks at the types of families produced by remarriage, in which virtual strangers suddenly find themselves part of a blended stepfamily. She explains how loving relationships can gradually develop in such families and the difficulties in adjusting to a stepfamily, particularly when a new family structure brings a change in lifestyle or new siblings.

In her article "Children of Two Faiths," April Austin highlights the difficulties couples face when they come from different religious backgrounds, particularly when they have children. Many interfaith couples choose to emphasize both traditions rather than favoring one, claiming that this approach teaches children that there is more than one way to view the universe. Austin also discusses the hardships of trying to maintain two religions in one household, and the difficult choices that children raised in such an atmosphere make when deciding if they should adopt one parent's faith over the other.

The report "AARP Survey: Boomer Population Redefines 'Sandwich Generation'" discusses the increased caretaking burden faced by many baby boomers. Members of this generation are often responsible not only for their children, but also their elderly parents, and in some cases extended family members, such as nieces, nephews, aunts, or uncles. Statistics are given for the amount of time different racial populations of baby boomers spend in caretaking duties and their attitudes towards the caretaking role.

In "Make Room for Granddaddy," Pamela Paul considers the changing roles of grandparents over the past few decades, especially how younger grandparents are shattering the stereotypes of the grandma and grandpa as retired and sedentary individuals. According to Paul, grandparents are spending more money than ever before on their grandkids, a fact that is coming to the attention of marketing executives. They are also more likely to work outside the home or be involved in community activities, thereby curtailing the amount of babysitting they are able to do. Nevertheless, grandparents are more engaged in their grandchildren's lives than ever before, planning activities together or living with their grandchildren (whether with or without a parent in the household). With their life spans increasing, grandparents can often become closer to their grandchildren than they would in the past and can have a greater impact on their lives in the long term.

The Adoption Maze[1]

By Kim Clark and Nancy Shute
U.S. News & World Report, March 12, 2001

What longing is strong enough to pull a person halfway around the globe for a rendezvous with a stranger? It drew Barbara and Randy Combs from their home in Frederick, Md., to a Siberian winter 12 time zones away. On February 21, they stood in Novosibirsk's Baby Home No. 2, looking for the first time at 9-month-old Viktoria Istomina, who stared solemnly back. The moment was oddly quiet, considering that it would change all their lives forever. "In the photos she had brown eyes," Barbara said, "but they're beautiful blue, blue-gray." Randy petted the child's back. "Look at that!" he said. "When you smiled, it pretty much made my day."

The Combses are among the tens of thousands of Americans who decide each year to adopt a child. Barbara, a 41-year-old accountant, and Randy, a 42-year-old computer systems engineer, had anticipated producing a sibling for their 3-year-old daughter, Jordyn. But a ruptured ectopic pregnancy that almost killed Barbara last February made that impossible. "I wasn't sure about adoption," Barbara says, "but Randy had no qualms whatsoever." By summer's end, Barbara had laid to rest her fear that she would favor her biological child over an adopted one. They knew right away they were going to Russia; friends had just adopted from there, Barbara's family had Russian roots, and she was convinced that no American birth mother would ever pick them, because they were over 40 and already had a child. "There are children out there," Barbara said. "Let's do it."

In the past 35 years, adoption has been transformed from a shameful family secret to a praiseworthy act—one that finds families for children, helps birthparents in desperate straits, and brings the blessing of parenthood to the childless. Because of rising infertility rates and increasing societal acceptance of gay and single parents, interest in adoption has skyrocketed. A survey of American women in 1988 found just 200,000 considering adoption. By 1995, the last year for which statistics are available, 500,000 wanted to adopt a child. But most want a healthy white infant, and the supply of those has plummeted. As a result, the number of Americans heading overseas to build their families has more than doubled in the past decade to more than 18,000 a year.

But just as society has become more accepting of adoption, the process has become more difficult, expensive, and potentially heartbreaking. Adoption has moved from the tightly self-regulated realm of social-service agencies and unwed mothers' homes to the free market. Babies are hawked on Web sites that trumpet "FEES REDUCED" for individuals such as Child No. 678, "deformed right hand but mentally fine and very sweet." Hundreds of for-profit businesses and unlicensed facilitators promise to connect prospective parents with the child of their dreams—with costs ranging from $15,000 to $50,000. "I used to say adoption has become a business," says Susan Soon-keum Cox, a vice president with Holt International Children's Services in Eugene, Ore. "Now I say it's become an industry."

> *Babies are hawked on Web sites that trumpet "FEES REDUCED."*

The infamous Internet twins case showed just how cutthroat the wild frontier of adoption can be. California facilitator Tina Johnson allegedly took $6,000 for placing the twins with a California couple, then turned the children over to a British couple for $12,000. The Britons whisked the children from California to Arkansas to take advantage of discrepancies in state laws and hurried them out of the country. The children are now in foster care in England while authorities sort out the sordid mess. And in thousands of less notorious cases, families struggle with a system that seems broken and ask: If adoption is so good, why does it have to be so hard?

Parents who want to adopt must make a dizzying array of choices—Which agency is reliable? Should they risk working with an unlicensed facilitator? Should they accept a child who may not be as healthy as claimed?—with little objective information to help them. And these families are increasingly likely to have their hearts broken and their bank accounts drained by a failed or fraudulent adoption. It was bad enough in 1990 when, insurance statistics show, fully 20 percent of families trying to adopt lost money to a birthparent's change of mind or a con artist. But by 1999 a heartbreaking 28 percent of insured adoptions failed.

Unprotected. To add insult to injury, adopting parents have surprisingly few rights. Scandals in the 19th and 20th centuries led to strong laws protecting children and birthparents, but there is virtually no protection for those wanting to adopt. State regulators across the country say they ignore most of the complaints against agencies because there are no rules requiring explanation of fees or accurate information about waiting lists, let alone refunds for a failed adoption.

It was perhaps inevitable that adoption would become more expensive and riskier. That tends to happen in any endeavor where there's an imbalance between supply and demand. In fact, when the supply of children exceeded demand in the mid-19th century, urban street children became a commodity; they were rounded up and sent west on "orphan trains," which would stop in farm towns where labor-hungry farmers would take their pick. Though some of the 84,000 orphan-train riders may have ended up in loving homes, many were abused.

But by 1950, demand for children started to outstrip the domestic supply, and in recent years the imbalance has become extreme. In 1988 there were 3.3 families looking for every adoption that was finalized. By 1995, there were 6, according to the National Survey of Family Growth. Of course, there has never been any shortage of adoptable children in the nation's foster care system (118,000 at last count). But red tape makes it difficult to pry those children loose. In addition, surveys consistently show that most adoptive families want healthy infants. Two thirds of foster care kids are at least 5 years old, and many have physical or emotional handicaps.

Race also plays a role. Although black and white women are equally likely to try to adopt, there are more white people in the population—and more black and mixed-race children in need of families. Of the adoptable children in foster care, 61 percent are black or Hispanic, and 32 percent are white. At the same time, the number of white infants placed for adoption has dropped, as single white women join black women in choosing to keep their children. A 1996 federal law makes it illegal for agencies to refuse to place a child with parents of another race, and transracial adoptions are on the rise, with celebrities such as Rosie O'Donnell adopting mixed-race children. But in 1998, only 15 percent of adoptions from foster care were transracial or transcultural. The disparity between the demand for white and black babies "is one of the saddest statements about adoption today," says Allan Hazlett, president of the American Academy of Adoption Attorneys.

The discrepancy between supply and demand has escalated adoption prices. Total spending on adoption is rising at 15 percent a year, hitting $1.4 billion in 2000. Although the Nebraska Children's Home Society provides free adoptions to state residents, most private domestic adoptions run from $6,000 to $30,000. Foreign adoptions run higher, starting at $15,000 for China to well over $20,000 for Guatemala. Randy and Barbara Combs figure it will have cost them $25,000 to $30,000 to adopt Viktoria, once travel costs are included. By far the biggest chunk, the $14,000 foreign fee, went to Frank Foundation Child Assistance International, a Washington, D.C.-based organization that is one of the largest locating children in Russia. In 1998, Frank made a profit of $937,515 on revenues of $4.1 million. Cofounder Nina Kostina earned $197,017. Many adoptive parents are deeply troubled by the vast sums of money they pay and the lack of accountability: "On Sunday I fly into Moscow with $12,000 in cash strapped to my person," says Karen Groth, a 37-year-old Air Force major and intelligence officer who's adopting a baby girl from Kazakhstan. "Where does all our money go?"

Enter the FBI. That kind of unaccounted-for money can't help but draw in a few people with less than pure intentions. Take the much-publicized case of Tina Johnson, the facilitator who is under investigation for placing the twins with two families. *U.S. News* has learned the FBI is investigating another case in which Johnson, who runs A Caring Heart facilitation service in San Diego, allegedly charged a family $11,900 but never found them a child. Johnson, who did not return calls and E-mail asking for comment, also runs a Web site with the address of *www.Iattractmoney.com*. There, she pitches get-rich-quick schemes and, until recently, identified herself as "Tina Devereaux, success consultant."

The lure of profit is turning the heads of some potential birth mothers as well. There are at least two former birth mothers in prison for promising their unborn children to several families at once and collecting living expenses from all of them. And adoption chat rooms are filled with sad tales of families who have paid for living and medical expenses, only to have the birth mother exercise her right to change her mind. But those stories give a bum rap to the vast majority of birth mothers. Studies of teen moms show that those who place their children for adoption tend to be older, better educated, and emotionally stronger than those who keep their children.

> *"I would tell anybody considering adoption to go international."*— Candy Murdock, victim of adoption scheme.

Still, prospective parents have few legal safeguards. Government officials rarely treat their complaints seriously. Bill Lee, Maryland's adoption licensing coordinator, says when he gets complaints from adoptive parents about money, he makes a courtesy investigative phone call but can do nothing more: "We toss 'em." The state's regulations don't cover such contract disputes, he explains. Other officials move, but glacially. In a lawsuit, Candy and Bob Murdock, a Georgia couple, allege they paid $11,000 in 1998 to Lorraine Boisselle, who ran a Mississippi adoption agency. Two years later, after they say Boisselle gave them increasingly outlandish explanations for her failure to find a child (she once blamed a hurricane), the Murdocks called the Mississippi attorney general's office. They say they were surprised to learn that there were already complaints pending and that Boisselle's license had lapsed. The state says it is still investigating Boisselle. The Murdocks have joined with two other victims in filing a civil suit in an attempt to recover their money. "There is no way you can protect yourself," Candy Murdock says. After her experience, "I would tell anybody considering adoption to go international."

Looking abroad. That's precisely what many people are deciding to do. Over the past 10 years, the number of children adopted from overseas has more than doubled, from 7,093 in 1990 to 18,441 last year, and the numbers are expected to keep rising. Foreign adoption became institutionalized in the 1950s after the Korean War, when

Americans began adopting orphans and Amerasian children. But the picture radically changed in the early 1990s. Images of gruesome Romanian orphanages sparked an international effort to rescue children there. The fall of communism in the Soviet bloc paved the way for adoption from Russia and its former republics. And China started allowing foreign adoption of the thousands of girls abandoned by a society that favors male offspring. China and Russia have now eclipsed South Korea as the top two sources of foreign adoptions in the United States, with Guatemala a close fourth. Hundreds of new agencies have sprung up to meet this increased demand.

But foreign adoption, even if it avoids some of the complications of domestic adoption, brings its own difficulties. Two countries' legal requirements must be met, two bureaucracies assuaged. "I applied for a job at the CIA once," Randy Combs recalls. "This was much more paperwork." All adoptions require a home study. Going international requires a dossier of documents for the foreign country and approval by the U.S. Immigration and Naturalization Service. Deanna Hodgin and Philip Dworsky have waited four months for INS approval of their petition to adopt an infant girl from Kazakhstan. Hodgin, a San Francisco communications manager, says she'll quit her job in mid-March and fly to Kazakhstan and wait there: "At least while I'm there I can see the baby each day, feed her some more-nutritious food, and try to improve her condition."

Guesswork. The most daunting, and potentially devastating, hurdle in international adoption is assessing a child's health in the face of incomplete or faulty medical information. Nobody wants to go through what Debbie and David Crick of Apison, Tenn., have. They adopted a boy they thought was 10 years old from the Republic of Georgia in 1996, only to find out he was actually 14 and seriously mentally ill. In the case of Randy and Barbara Combs, the couple know nothing about their daughter's birth father and little more about her birth mother, a 20-year-old shop clerk who left the newborn at the maternity hospital. Prospective parents typically receive a short video of a child and a synopsis of the medical history. Little Viktoria's analysis included neurological terms like "pyramidal insufficiency" and "perinatal encephalopathy." "It's very scary," says Barbara. The Combses took their video and report to a pediatrician, and also called the orphanage's doctor with the help of a translator. "She's good kind baby," the doctor said. The couple started packing for Siberia.

Most children coming to the United States are from countries like Russia with poor medical systems, where pregnant women often get no prenatal care and are malnourished. Children adopted from abroad also often suffer ailments that a suburban pediatrician wouldn't even think to look for, including syphilis, tuberculosis, intestinal parasites, and hepatitis B and C.

Those health problems are exacerbated in orphanages, where children are often underfed and the lack of individual attention delays physical and mental development. In a study published last year, 75 percent of children adopted from China had significant developmental delays. (Korea and Guatemala are considered exceptions, because children are placed in foster care instead of in orphanages and usually get good medical care.) "These kids are high risk," says Ronald Federici, an Alexandria, Va., neuropsychologist who treats foreign adoptees. Many agencies, he says, require parents to sign liability waivers, which absolve the agency of responsibility if the child later turns out to have serious medical or psychological problems.

Indeed, Frank Foundation's Nina Kostina says that parents need to be ready to bail out: "When the parents are in the orphanage with the medical records in front of them, this is the time. Call your pediatrician in the United States. This is a lifetime decision."

Given the emotional investment, that's not easy. Barbara Combs says she doesn't think she would have had the strength to say no once she'd made it all the way to Novosibirsk, after an overnight flight from Moscow. Fortunately, she felt she didn't have to. The

---

"Considering you're going to another country and taking guardianship of another human being, it's been amazingly smooth."—Randy **Combs, adoptive parent.**

---

medical information from the orphanage doctor matched what she'd heard before, aside from a "peculiarity of the coccyx." The translator started dictating a letter to the court, as Randy wrote longhand: "We have met the child and bonded with her. We are aware of her health concerns."

Heading home. Two days later, Barbara and Randy were standing before a Siberian judge, who after 40 minutes of questions declared that Viktoria Nikolaevna Istomina was now Victoria Nicole Combs. Three days later, the sleep-deprived family was on the plane for home, surrounded by other adoptive parents with wailing babies. Victoria was diagnosed with a mild case of rickets due to lack of vitamin D, and her family doctor said the "peculiarity of the coccyx" dismissed by the orphanage doctor may require surgery. But her exhausted parents remain pleased. "Considering you're going to another country and taking guardianship of another human being," Randy says, "it's been amazingly smooth."

Just last Tuesday, Victoria made history as she and about 75,000 other children adopted from abroad instantly became American citizens, thanks to the Childhood Citizenship Act of 2000, designed so that foreign adoptees would not risk being deported if their parents failed to have them naturalized. Children adopted abroad now become citizens once they enter the States. That, and pending legislation that would raise the federal tax credit for adoption from $5,000 to $10,000 per child, are hailed by adoptive parents and advocates as significant steps toward encouraging adoption. The third step is more significant still—the Hague Convention on Intercountry Adoption. Last year, after a decade of effort, Congress approved legislation to implement the international treaty, which is designed to stop trafficking in children and promote international adoption. For the first time, the United States will have a central authority that will accredit adoption agencies and a federal database. "If there are enough complaints about an agency, that agency could be removed," says Mary Marshall, director of the Office of Children's Issues at the State Department. It will take up to three years for the central authority to be created, but once it's online, prospective parents will have for the first time a central source of information on agencies, one that should prove useful to parents adopting domestically as well.

In the meantime, adoption advocates say parents should use their heads, not just their hearts, when seeking a child. "If you were buying a car, you wouldn't plunk down your $45,000 without looking it up in *Consumer Reports*," says Jerri Jenista, an Ann Arbor, Mich., pediatrician who has been practicing adoption medicine for 20 years and who has adopted five children from India. "I see people who adopt a child for the same amount of money with zero preparation. You have to do your homework."

The Reappearing Nuclear Family[2]

BY DAVID BLANKENHORN
FIRST THINGS, JANUARY 2002

As if it didn't have enough to fret about, the two-parent American family got taken for quite a ride in the past year. First, in April the Census Bureau dramatically reported that the "nuclear family" was "rebounding." The page-one story in *USA Today* announced: "The traditional nuclear family—a married mom and dad living with their biological children—is making a comeback, according to a Census report released today. The proportion of the nation's children living with both biological parents jumped from 51 percent in 1991 to 56 percent . . . in 1996." On *ABC World News Tonight*, Peter Jennings declared: "The Census Bureau said today that the number of children who live with both their parents increased during the 1990s." Scores of news organizations around the country reported the same happy story.

But in May, the story reversed itself. Journalists across the country began to report that "nuclear families" now constitute less than 25 percent of all U.S. households. An editorial in the *New York Post* announced that "the American nuclear family" was now "up there with the Pacific salmon as an endangered species." A *Newsweek* cover story on unmarried mothers ("the new faces of America's family album") explained at length how the "traditional family" was "fading fast." Dr. James Dobson, the radio personality and president of Focus on the Family, an influential Christian pro-family organization, said that the "alarming" Census Bureau figures revealed "just how dire the situation has become," as "the family is unraveling at a faster pace than ever." The *New York Times* took a sunnier view. Following up on its page-one news story ("Number of Nuclear Families Drops as 1-Parent Families Rise"), the *Times* editorial board urged its readers not to worry about the decline, since "the nuclear family is not the only kind of family or even the only healthy kind of family."

Well, now. Is it possible for the nuclear family to be simultaneously "making a comeback" and "fading fast"? Of course not. So which is true? Amazingly enough, the answer is *neither*. What is actually happening to U.S. family structure is quite different from the news conveyed by either cycle of stories.

While the Census Bureau has been quick to blame the media for the confusion, the fault lies primarily with the Bureau. For mysterious reasons, the Census Bureau chose in the fine print of its April

2. Article by David Blankenhorn from *First Things* January 2002. Copyright © *First Things*. Reprinted with permission.

report to define a "traditional nuclear family" as a household consisting of two biological parents, their minor children, *and no one else.* That is, a household that includes grandparents is not "traditional." A household that includes boarders, or a foster child, is not "traditional." Moreover, during the 1990s, for reasons that have almost nothing to do with the core issue—which is how many U.S. children are growing up in households with two married parents—three-generation and large or complex households with children declined slightly as a proportion of all households with children.

That little curio of a demographic fact—that tangent of a tangent—was the entire basis of the Census Bureau's April "rebound" report. No evidence presented in that report justifies the assertion that the proportion of children living with both biological parents rose during the early- and mid-1990s. And to add injury to insult, the obscurantist definition of "traditional" means that the Census Bureau, while allegedly describing a nuclear family "rebound," actually *underreported* the proportion of U.S. children living with two married parents. The Census Bureau report puts the figure at 56 percent for 1996. But my own research, subsequently confirmed

---

During the 1990s, . . . three-generation and large or complex households with children declined slightly as a proportion of all households with children.

---

by other researchers and the Census Bureau itself, shows that the actual figure for 1996 is 64 percent.

As for May's precipitous drop in optimism, it can be traced to further manipulation of definitions on the part of journalists with no helpful guidance and arguably even some complicity from the Census Bureau. This time, using a data table released in mid-May with much fanfare by the Census Bureau, journalists chose to measure married-couple-with-children families not as a proportion of all *families* (two or more persons living together related by blood, marriage, or adoption), but instead as a proportion of all *households.* Grandma living on her own is a household. College roommates sharing an apartment are a household. The number of non-family households in the U.S. has been growing steadily for many decades for multiple reasons (including longer life spans and greater affluence), most of which have little to do with the state of marriage and child rearing. Indeed, marrieds-with-children were a distinct minority of all U.S. *households* even in the 1950s. That's why most scholars agree that the best way to measure the prevalence of a family phenomenon such as marriage is to place it in the context of family households; throwing in non-family households is like mixing apples and oranges. This piece of confusion was the primary basis for the "decline" stories that received so much attention last May.

This episode is a distressing example of irresponsibility by a public agency charged with collecting and reporting data on how we live. Even at this late date, it is impossible for scholars to get accurate trend-line data from the Census Bureau on the proportion of U.S. children living with their two biological married parents. This past June, nine senior family scholars, led by Norval Glenn of the University of Texas and Linda Waite of the University of Chicago, wrote a public letter to the Census Bureau asking it to disentangle the definitions and report this basic information. The Census Bureau politely declined. For the time being, at least, accurate information about this trend will have to come from elsewhere.

Which brings us to the truly good news. A series of recent reports from independent scholars, plus largely unpublished data from the 2000 Census, all suggest that the trend of family fragmentation that many analysts had assumed to be unstoppable suddenly stopped in its tracks about six years ago.

What we are seeing is not (at least not yet) a "rebound." But it's certainly not a "decline." To be conservative, let's call it a cessation, a significant pause. But let's say it more optimistically: after more than three decades of relentless advance, the family structure revolution in the U.S. may be over.

Here are the basic numbers. The proportion of all U.S. families with children under age eighteen that are headed by married couples reached an all-time low in the mid 1990s—about 72.9 percent in 1996 and 72.4 percent in 1997—but has since stabilized. The figure for 2000 is 73 percent. Similarly, the proportion of all U.S. children living in two-parent homes reached an all-time low in the mid-1990s, but since then has stabilized as well. In fact, the proportion of children in two-parent homes increased slightly from 68 percent in 1999 to 69.1 percent in 2000.

Looking only at white, non-Hispanic children, a study by Allan Dupree and Wendell Primus finds that the proportion of these children living with two married parents stopped its downward descent during the late 1990s, and even increased modestly from 1999 to 2000, rising from 77.3 to 78.2 percent. Another study from the Urban Institute finds that, among all U.S. children, the proportion living with their two biological or adoptive parents increased by 1.2 percent from 1997 to 1999, while during the same period the proportion living in stepfamilies (or blended families) decreased by 0.1 percentage points and the proportion living in single-parent homes decreased by two percentage points. (The study finds that in 1999 about 64 percent of all U.S. children lived with their two biological or adoptive parents, while about 25 percent lived with one parent and about 8 percent lived in a step or blended family.) Among low-income children, the decline in the proportion living in single-parent homes was even more pronounced, dropping from 44 percent in 1997 to 41 percent in 1999.

And, perhaps most encouraging, from 1995 to 2000 the proportion of African-American children living in two-parent, married-couple homes rose from 34.8 to 38.9 percent, a significant increase in just five years, representing the clear cessation and even reversal of the long-term shift toward black family fragmentation.

What has caused this shift? No one knows for sure, but we can make some plausible guesses. The roaring economy probably had little or nothing to do with it, since all previous economic booms since 1970 have coincided with growing family fragmentation, not reintegration. On the other hand, federal and state welfare reforms dating from the mid-1990s, which dramatically restructured and in some instances eliminated what had previously been guaranteed economic supports for unmarried mothers, have almost certainly played a role. As the above-cited data suggest, post-1995 family structure changes have been most dramatic among low-income families.

More generally, on the core social question of whether family fragmentation is a bad thing or a not-so-bad thing, a steady shift in popular and (especially) elite opinion took place over the course of the 1990s. Denial and happy talk about the consequences of nuclear family decline became decidedly less widespread; concern and even alarm became much more common. As a society we changed our minds, and as a result we changed some of our laws. And now, it seems, we are beginning to change some of our personal behavior. This is very encouraging news.

It is now clear that those who have long and loudly insisted that nothing can be done to stop the trend of family fragmentation are wrong. Remember all their clichés? We have to be realistic, they opined. The "family diversity" trend is irreversible. We can't put the toothpaste back in the tube. We shouldn't fall into the "nostalgia trap." We can't go back to "Ozzie and Harriet." Well, the next time someone tells you that, just smile and show him the new numbers. Positive change in U.S. family structure is not only desirable and possible. It is already occurring. Today our main challenge is no longer to reverse a trend toward disintegration, but to intensify the nascent trend toward reintegration.

Step by Step[3]

BY ROBERTA ISRAELOFF
PARENTS, AUGUST 1996

"I'd be in the middle of cooking dinner, madly trying to get everything ready and on the table," recalls Diane Shaw, a doctor's receptionist in Westfield, Connecticut, "and my stepdaughter would walk in, take a look around, and say, 'My mom never made that for dinner!'"

Jan Scharman, a psychology professor at Brigham Young University, in Salt Lake City, remembers the difficult weekend mornings when her seven stepdaughters would visit. "They'd adoringly surround their father in the kitchen. Standing across the room from them, I could have been in Siberia. I felt as if I was there only to take their breakfast orders."

Just about every stepparent has endured times like these, moments that made them wonder whether their new families would ever work. It often seems that when adults remarry, children go out of their way to act in a hurtful, hostile manner that grown-ups can't help taking personally.

But parents and stepparents must try to understand that behind every hurtful comment and hostile action is a child who is scared, and who is desperately trying to get her needs met, says Patricia Papernow, Ed.D., author of *Becoming a Stepfamily* (Jossey-Bass).

Stepchildren, like all kids, need to feel loved and accepted. They need a sense of belonging and some sense of control over their own lives, notes Emily Visher, Ph.D., cofounder of the Stepfamily Association of America and author of *How to Win as a Stepfamily* (Brunner-Mazel). But the emotional and physical upheavals of remarriage can undermine these needs.

Of course, how well a child adjusts to a parent's remarriage depends on factors such as the child's age and developmental stage; whether the remarriage follows death or divorce; the quality of the relationship between the adults; and whether other children are involved.

How can you help kids cope with all these factors? Experts say that in successful stepfamilies, parents and stepparents ease the transition by understanding the children's point of view—which involves being patient and helping kids talk about their feelings—and by keeping adult conflicts at a low level.

The Idea of Remarriage Is Threatening to Kids

For adults, remarriage is a joyful, hopeful beginning—an opportunity to create a new family after death or divorce shattered the first.

But for children, it is merely another change thrust upon them after a long series of changes. "One night shortly after I remarried, I sat on the porch with my 9-year-old stepdaughter," recalls Scharman. "I was thrilled about the wedding, relieved to finally be living with Brent. But when I tried talking to my stepdaughter, she started to cry and couldn't stop. She was scared by so many things, and tired of all the upheaval."

Jeannette Lofas, founder of the Stepfamily Foundation and coauthor, with Dawn B. Sova, of *Stepparenting* (Kensington Books), explains, "Kids want the opposite of what adults want. They're not interested in a new family; they want their old family back. They generally don't care about gaining a stepfather; they're scared about losing their mother to him. Finally, remarriage deals a crushing, fatal blow to the child's most fervent wish—that her parents will get back together again."

> *"Remarriage deals a crushing, fatal blow to the child's most fervent wish—that her parents will get back together again."*
> —Jeannette Lofas, founder of the Stepfamily Foundation.

By knowing ahead of time why children act the way they do, parents and stepparents will be better prepared to understand and resolve any problems that might arise.

Expect regression in toddlers. Because very young children are less set in their ways, they may adapt more easily to remarriage than older kids. But it's not uncommon for them to register their distress at the changes in their lives by regressing. "If the remarriage occurs soon after your 2 1/2-year-old daughter was toilet-taught, don't be surprised if she goes back to wanting diapers," notes Visher. Nursery-school-age children are also likely to throw tantrums, change eating and sleeping patterns, and cling to their own parent.

"The best way to help children this age cope with the myriad changes," says Visher, "is to keep their routine as stable as possible, and to be especially loving and attentive." To preserve this stability, toddlers—like all kids—also need to maintain a close relationship with the noncustodial parent.

Since young children may have difficulty grasping stepfamily issues, such as visitation schedules, Visher suggests developing visual ways to help them. For example, use colored markers on a special calendar to indicate the days they'll be spending with each parent.

Children 4 to 7 may have feelings of displacement. Order and control are important to kids in this age group, and they react strongly to the physical disruptions that occur in the early life of a stepfamily. For example, when the Shaws married, Diane and her 4-year-old daughter moved into Tony's house, which proved hard on everyone. "Tony's preteen daughters felt as if they'd been invaded by strangers," Diane recalls. At the same time, her daughter had to acclimate herself to a whole new household. "If I had to do it again," Diane says, "I'd have both families move into a new house—one that was ours."

But even in a wholly new environment, children in stepfamilies feel possessive—of their toys, their room—and vulnerable to feelings of displacement. When John and Cindy Stasko, of North Haven, Connecticut, were married, John's youngest daughter was no longer the baby of the family. Not only did she have a new sister, but all the expectations of being an older child also fell on her shoulders for the first time.

To help children feel a sense of belonging, Visher suggests that families find ways to give them pockets of control. "You can tell your son that he can't hog the whole couch when his stepsister wants to watch TV with him, but you can ask him on which end he'd like to sit," she says. To adults such a choice seems trivial, but children appreciate having options.

It's also a good idea, says Papernow, to let each child make decisions about family activities. "Give everyone a turn at choosing what to eat for dinner on Sunday nights and what video to watch afterward," she suggests. This goes a long way toward making them feel like valued members of the family.

Kids 8 to 12 may try to test your love. Though all children are concerned with issues of fairness and loyalty, kids of this age may be more acutely aware of them. They tend to see things in terms of black and white. Most children have trouble understanding that they can belong to two families at the same time. The acceptance of a stepparent may seem to be a rejection of their own parent, and any attachment to the stepparent could be perceived as disloyalty. Experts say it's extremely helpful if both parents tell their child, "We know you love us, but it's okay to love your stepparent too."

It's also typical for 8- to 12-year-olds to try to test your love by forcing you to choose between them and your new partner. In early adolescence, this behavior can have a rivalrous edge. "I'd be sitting on the couch watching television with my husband," explains Ellen Ostrow, a Washington, D.C., area psychologist, "and my 12-year-old stepdaughter would sit on the floor between us and put her hand on my husband's leg."

The solution? "Ideally, the father should speak to his daughter privately and let her know that such gestures aren't appropriate," says Papernow. "At the same time, he needs to acknowledge that she's probably expressing her need to spend more one-on-one time with him, and he should suggest that they do so—while also making it clear that he needs one-on-one time with his new partner as well."

A stepparent must make her feelings known. If the father ignores his daughter's provocative behavior, the stepmother must speak with him about it. "Bring it up in a calm, nonblaming way," suggests Papernow. "Begin by saying, 'We need to talk about something. You may not be aware of it, but your daughter acts possessively toward you. It makes me feel awkward. I'd like it if you'd tell her not to act like that anymore when we are all together.'" This approach—which thoughtfully acknowledges your partner's feelings and includes a clear request—usually gets results.

Who Should Play the Bad Guy?

Discipline is a thorny problem for many new stepfamilies. Developing a strategy that suits both parents takes time—a luxury that many stepparents don't have. At the same time, because of all the changes going on around them, the kids are acting out more than ever. As a result, both parent and stepparent agree that more discipline is needed, yet no one is sure who should apply it, when it should take place, or how much is enough.

"Most kids are less than thrilled to have a stranger disciplining them," says Patricia Papernow, Ed.D. She advises that each parent discipline his own children whenever possible, and that a stepparent think of her role as an aunt or baby-sitter—someone who's in charge until the real authority gets home.

But this doesn't mean that stepparents can't speak up when kids act out. "A stepparent has the right to expect civil behavior from stepchildren," says Papernow, and she should let them know when they get out of line. If the child answers back by saying, "You're not my mother," the best response is, "Yes, that's right. And these are the rules of the house, and I'm going to hold you to them."

Some stepfamilies, however, take a less restrictive approach. In the Stasko household, in North Haven, Connecticut, both parents feel equally responsible for disciplining all the kids. As Cindy Stasko explains, "Whoever sees the bad behavior addresses it." Since she tends to be home with the kids more often than her husband, Cindy does most of the disciplining, and has no problem with her role.

"The key to success when it comes to discipline is feeling as if you and your husband are on the same page," she says. "As long as you agree on discipline, it doesn't matter who administers it."

However, other situations might call for a stepparent to be assertive without expecting help from her spouse. "My first Christmas as a stepmom," recalls Ostrow, "we were all exchanging gifts when my stepdaughter blithely said, 'Oh, guess what? I forgot to get you a present.'"

In this scenario, everyone is placed in a difficult spot. "I understood my stepdaughter's gesture to mean two things: He's mine, and you don't belong here. Naturally, I wanted my husband to rush to my defense, to say that not only did I belong in the family, but that I was very important."

But if her husband had spoken up, he would have widened a split he was trying to heal. As the person in the middle, he didn't want to hurt his wife or daughter.

Ultimately, Ostrow says, she waited a few days until her anger subsided. "I then took my stepdaughter aside and said, 'It really hurt my feelings that you didn't get me a present. I understand that I haven't been a member of the family for very long, and if you'd like to tell me your feelings about it, I'd be happy to listen.' My stepdaughter replied, 'I didn't mean anything by it. I was just very busy and forgot.'"

At that moment, says Ostrow, there was nothing else to say. "The most important thing was that I let her know how hurt I was—but it was the last time I was not given a Christmas gift."

All Children Need Individual Attention from Parents

A good way to heal loyalty issues—and to foster a sense of belonging in stepchildren of any age—is for each child and adult in the family to spend time together, advises Papernow. "This helps stepfamilies get over the feeling that someone is always an outsider." Naturally, parents need to spend special time with their own children, but the step relationship also needs tending.

"Even 15 minutes a day with a stepchild helps," Papernow says. In the beginning, "shoulder to shoulder" time—when you're doing something together like shopping or cooking—may feel much more comfortable than an intimate, one-on-one talk. Or offer to teach your stepchild something you're good at, suggests Papernow. "Concentrating on an activity, something besides the relationship itself, helps defuse the tension you're both feeling," she says.

Adult–child conflicts are not the only ones that need attention. Grown-ups should try to maintain harmony in their own relationships. Experts say that kids who are exposed to a barrage of parental battles can have a more difficult time adjusting to remarriage. Regardless of how much anger (justified or not) you might feel toward a noncustodial parent, never criticize him within earshot of your child. "Kids identify strongly with their parents," Papernow explains. "If your son hears you say, 'My ex-husband is a jerk,' your son will feel as if you're saying that he's a jerk." As one 7-year-old boy notes, "It feels like all the adults are shooting arrows at each other, and they all go right through me."

In the End, the Hard Work Is Worth the Struggle

No matter how much you try, the process of becoming a stepfamily often seems terribly daunting. Diane Shaw remembers going for a walk one night about a year after she remarried. "It was a very low point for me. Becoming a stepmother was much harder than I had anticipated. I couldn't help asking myself, Did I do the right thing? Is this really what I want? If Tony dies before me, will I even have an emotional attachment to his daughters?"

Nine years later, she feels very different. "During a conversation with the girls the other night, they told me that they couldn't imagine their dad with anyone else. They said we showed them what a good relationship was all about. I was so gratified. It's been a rocky ride, but we love each other. We made it."

"Where Do I Fit In?"

Stepchildren Struggle to Feel at Home in New Families.

Michelle, 8

"There are different rules at my mom's house than at my dad's. One thing is, I don't have to wash my hands before dinner at my mom's, but I do at my dad's. It's hard to keep track sometimes.

"The hardest part when your parents are divorced is going back and forth between two houses. It takes about an hour, or at least it seems like an hour, to get to my dad's and then back. That's really a pain.

"I don't like to see my dad and Anita [my stepmother] fight. I feel really bad when that happens. And sometimes I feel stuck in the middle when my dad fights with my mom."

Alex, 9

"I've been in a stepfamily since I was 6 years old. The thing I regret most is my parents' divorce. I don't like it when they fight. I'm always put in the middle, like a messenger. They got divorced when I was 3, and it became official on my birthday—some birthday present!

"If I had one wish, it would be that my dad, my stepmother, and my mom were all good friends. A girl in my class has divorced parents, but they still have dinner together.

"My stepmom is a decent person. She's not like some evil witch. She's someone I can talk to if I'm having a problem. The best thing about my stepfamily is my new baby sister. She's great!"

Cole, 11

"[In a stepfamily] you have two of a lot of things. And it's kind of nice that your parents have more time with you and like to be with you because they don't see you as much.

"It's really hard when you want to be with both parents and you're always missing one. It's kind of sad because your family has broken up and you're feeling, you know, sad.

"It really works to have a [visitation] schedule. Then you don't have to choose who to be with, and it gives you a feeling of security."

Adam, 17

"My stepfather cares more about his biological children—my half-brother and half-sister—than he does about me.

"Whenever I fight with one of them he always takes their side, and my mom has to defend me. It's as if they choose up sides based on biology.

"Because of my stepfamily, I have an 18-year-old cousin in Florida. We talk on the phone, and I visited him last year. It's interesting, meeting new people. My stepfather's family welcomed me, which I really appreciated."

Ashlie, 16

"Being part of a stepfamily is a good thing, really. I've been very lucky: I get along great with my sister and my half-brother.

"It's like everyone can have the best of both worlds. When I visit my dad, my stepmother doesn't have children of her own, but she has us!

"My father remarried and moved far away. My grandmother gave him and my stepmother a subscription to my hometown paper because my sister and I are involved in a lot of sports. They can see our pictures in there when we're featured, so he feels closer."

Ethan, 14

"The hardest part of being in a stepfamily is having to listen to my stepfather. He is so strict. My mom wasn't like that before she married him; we used to do things together and she was more relaxed.

"Now I have to obey his rules, and it's hard. I can't even leave my jacket on the couch for five minutes before he's yelling at me to put it away. I hate that.

"In my situation, the bad parts definitely outweigh the good."

Luke, 12

"The good part about stepfamilies is that you meet a lot of new people; your family multiplies fast, especially if your stepparent has kids. I like that.

"It's fun to have a little brother. He's my half-brother, actually, and he really looks up to me. I'm teaching him how to do tricks on the skateboard, which is cool.

"It's hard to have a stepfather, because you just don't really know him. Besides, you're used to your regular dad. I used to feel uncomfortable around my stepfather sometimes when he first moved in.

"If you can, try to release stress by keeping busy. I like to skateboard and I also paint and do sculpture. That helps me relax when things get rough at home."

Children of Two Faiths[4]

By April Austin
The Christian Science Monitor, December 23, 1998

Growing up as the daughter of a Christian mother and a Jewish father, Ruth Lednicer says she loved Christmas—or at least the tinsel and trappings.

She had little idea that it had to do with Jesus. But "I developed strict rituals around the holiday, forcing my poor dad to read 'The Night Before Christmas' every Christmas Eve, with stockings hung a certain way," she says.

This despite the fact that her father had been a Jewish refugee from World War II.

"It was a bit confusing in adolescence," she says of December at the Lednicer house in Evansville, Ind., "feeling you weren't quite sure where you fit in."

These emotions are common in families where parents come from two different religious backgrounds, and there is evidence that the number of such families is growing. How parents handle the December holidays is one barometer of how successful they are the rest of the year in bridging their faiths and giving children a clear sense of identity. The stakes are high: Divorce rates are said to be higher for interfaith couples than for those of similar backgrounds; families often have difficulty finding a supportive religious community that doesn't have an agenda.

For some interfaith families, it's easier to keep harmony by not getting too specific with the theology.

Karen McCarthy, a psychologist in the Denver area, is a Roman Catholic married to a Jew. She and her husband have a three-year-old, and they're educating her in both religious traditions. "We try not to get hung up on the 'Jesus as God' part," she says, "instead we emphasize what Jesus' life was about, and the commonality in both our religions, such as the importance of being a good person."

That approach works best for Jewish-Christian couples, whose beliefs, at the core, are similar. In fact, Jewish-Christian matches are the most common interfaith relationships in North America. Jewish organizations estimate that 40 to 50 percent of Jews marry non-Jews.

Mixed marriage is rarer for devout Muslims, according to Ibrahim Hooper of the Council on Islamic Relations in Washington. Men may marry Jewish or Christian women with the expectation that children will be raised Muslim, but Muslim women are expected to marry inside the faith.

Intermarriage that involves Hinduism and Buddhism—two Eastern teachings that are less familiar to Westerners and may be less accessible because of language barriers—is still unusual but is more accepted than a generation ago.

Hindus and Buddhists are not as rigid on dogma as most Christian denominations, and where Christians see one path to godliness—through Christ—"Hindu philosophy acknowledges all paths to God as equal," says Anup Pandey of Albany, N.Y.

Mr. Pandey, who was born in India, and his American wife, Stacy Morris, were married in two ceremonies—Hindu and Roman Catholic. When the priest asked the couple beforehand what their children would be, Pandey told him: "They will be both—or all."

That kind of openness and optimism can carry an interfaith couple through the early years of marriage and past the first holidays—until children come along. Then parents often run smack into the realities of conflicting traditions.

Interfaith families say that the holidays go more smoothly if they focus on the children, and if parents fight the urge to recapture specific traditions from their own childhoods. Several families interviewed said that, when kids got older, it helped to have a pre-holiday family meeting to talk about expectations, discuss what worked and didn't from the previous year, and to get a feeling for how the children's religious ideas had matured since last holiday season.

The hard reality of interfaith families at the holidays is that it's often exhausting for the parents: They get worn out going to church, going to temple, cooking and decorating for two sets of holidays and entertaining two sets of families. As Eileen Smith, a Catholic married to a Jew in Chicago, puts it, "We don't do soccer, we do religion."

For many families, going the "both" route, as Ms. Smith's family does, is simply not feasible. They opt for an amalgam of traditions and customs, or seek neutral ground in a Unitarian-Universalist church. Others make the hard decision to emphasize a single religious teaching in the home. Interestingly, in quite a number of interfaith families, the Christian partner agrees to raise the children as Jewish, or the children themselves choose Judaism.

Mary Rosenbaum, a Catholic married to a Jew, is executive director of the Dovetail Institute for Interfaith Family Resources. She explains that it's easier for a Christian to accept Judaism than the other way around. "There isn't anything in Jewish prayers or symbols that Christians would oppose, since Christianity grew out of Judaism."

For children, the issue is more complicated. Ms. Lednicer says she is still straddling the fence. "To choose one faith over the other is to deny one side of my family and potentially hurt one parent. Given how much of my father's family was killed in the Holocaust, I feel a duty to carry on a tradition that survived despite attempts to quash it," she says. "It would be a shame if it all fell by the wayside because we couldn't be bothered to keep it alive."

With religion being such serious business, it's not easy for parents and kids to lighten up. Elizabeth Marvin is a first-year student at Illinois State University. Her mom was raised a Christian and her dad is Jewish. The family worships together at synagogue, but they also decorate for Christmas—with a touch of humor, Ms. Marvin says. "Our tree is topped with a Star of David, and we have other ornaments such as a plastic bagel and a figure from 'Fiddler on the Roof.' We all have stockings—only my dad's is blue and white and says 'Shalom,' instead of being red-and-white with a reindeer."

Adult children of interfaith families say that, despite the chal-

---

"Our tree is topped with a Star of David, and we have other ornaments such as a plastic bagel and a figure from 'Fiddler on the Roof.'"—**Elizabeth Marvin, child of interfaith marriage.**

---

lenges, they wouldn't trade their upbringing for anything. "I loved being from a mixed-religion household," says Rachel Maurer of Albuquerque, N.M. "Sure, at times I felt like a misfit, but I think it broadened my outlook and allowed me to cross social boundaries that other people cannot."

Marvin echoes those comments. "I'm not so threatened by other people asserting their religious beliefs," she says.

Taking their cue from parents, children of interfaith families often glide in and out of different religious realms with the ease of a bilingual person switching between two languages, says Smith. They realize, she says, "that there is not one language or one way to the Almighty."

Kate and Micahla Cohen, the teenage daughters of a Christian mother and a Jewish father in Minneapolis, say they feel fortunate to have two perspectives on religion. "I like that I can talk about both," Micahla says, although she has chosen Judaism and is studying for her bat mitzvah. A bar or bat mitzvah is a rite of passage that includes reading the Torah and taking one's place in the Jewish community.

Ms. McCarthy the psychologist says, "We do well when we ask ourselves, 'What's good for our daughter?' It's important to send a clear, consistent message of love and support whatever you choose to do, especially during the holidays."

"Faith is a gift," says Smith. "We can't dictate how children arrive at it, we can only give them the tools."

AARP Survey: Boomer Population Redefines "Sandwich Generation"[5]

PR NEWSWIRE, JULY 11, 2001

The Boomer population has redefined yet another aspect of American society—the "sandwich generation," according to a survey released today by AARP.

The sandwich generation label has been used for decades to describe those who provide care for both their children and their parents. But, reflecting new realities, the latest sandwich—as seen by AARP and increasingly embraced by leading experts and interest groups—extends the label to those likely to be managing the needs of immediate and extended family, and even those not related by blood.

The AARP survey has important multicultural findings, including the fact that large numbers of Asian Americans, Hispanic Americans, and African Americans provide care for parents and other adults.

"In today's multicultural America, we see new, nonnuclear family arrangements that find many Boomers sandwiched between extended family and nonfamily members," said Bill Novelli, AARP's executive director. "Caregivers today may be assisting not only their own children and parents, but also grandchildren, nieces, nephews, and even children of friends and neighbors."

Novelli outlined the new sandwich and its implications today as AARP released the results of the study—"In the Middle: A Report of Multicultural Boomers Coping with Family and Aging Issues"—the first report of its kind to document the attitudes and behavior of the sandwich generation from a multicultural perspective.

The national survey, conducted by telephone this spring with more than 2,300 Americans aged 45 to 55, found that many are squeezed, but not overwhelmed by the sandwich issue. Seventy-four percent say that they are able to handle their family responsibilities, and most say that they do not feel overly stressed by family issues.

However, some are beginning to feel the strain of having elderly parents and/or young children simultaneously—especially those who are directly responsible for the care of their parents and other older family members. Two in ten said they experience stress because they are sandwiched between older and younger generations, and three in ten who have responsibility for their parents' or in-laws' care cited stress.

---

5. Reprinted with permission from the American Association of Retired Persons (AARP).

"Low-income individuals . . . feel more stressed about their responsibilities and are less able to take time off work to help care for family members," the AARP report said. "Individuals with low incomes also report being more overwhelmed by their family responsibilities."

"It is significant that nearly one third—most notably, Asian Americans, Hispanic Americans, and African Americans, especially those with low incomes—feel heavily burdened," said Novelli. "Creative approaches are needed to help reduce that burden."

The report shows that the degree of participation, the ways in which the sandwich Boomers cope, and the dynamics of their families differ to some degree depending on race, culture, and income.

For example, Asian American and Hispanic American families feel more guilt about the level of care they provide, though, at the same time, they provide more care.

Nineteen percent of non-Hispanic whites participate in caring for parents and other older adults, compared with 28 percent of African Americans, 34 percent of Hispanic Americans, and 42 percent of Asian Americans. People born outside the United States are more likely to provide such care (43 percent) than those born in this country (20 percent).

Most members of the newly redefined sandwich generation welcome the chance to help care for their parents despite the added demands. But a sizable number—48 percent—believe they should be doing, or should have done, more for their parents. Asian Americans, among the most active caregivers, express the most guilt (72 percent), while the figure for Hispanic Americans is 65 percent and, for African Americans, 54 percent. Non-Hispanic whites feel less guilty (44 percent).

Despite their own family responsibilities, nearly 7 in 10 of all respondents (69%) rejected the idea that their children should be expected to take care of them in their old age. However, opinions on this issue vary by race and ethnicity, with non-Hispanic whites (72 percent) and African Americans (68 percent) least likely to expect care by their children. The figure for Hispanic Americans was 60 percent; for Asian Americans, 49 percent.

Contrasts are evident among the racial and ethnic groups, but so are similarities. All are coping, and a majority turn first to faith and prayer for comfort. Overall, the AARP survey found that, to help take care of family members, nearly two thirds (62 percent) of the sandwich generation turn to faith and prayer. Forty-two percent indicated that their church, synagogue, temple or other religious organization has been helpful.

Here are some other racial and ethnic highlights by group:

- Asian Americans (four percent of the sandwich generation) express more stress than others from pressures of caring for family members, with a high percentage (see above) providing more for their parents than are other Americans. Much of their caregiving is extremely time consuming, the survey found.

- Hispanic Americans (nine percent of the sandwich cohort) have more children than others and, more often, have both parents living. Over a third (34 percent) take responsibility for the care of parents and older relatives, and their commitment is frequently substantial: financial support, personal care, and helping obtain medical attention.

- African Americans (11 percent) deal with more potentially stressful situations than other groups, but with just as much optimism. Their coping mechanisms are likely to include religious faith, family connections (including siblings), and a greater reliance on doctors and governmental agencies than do other ethnic groups.

- Non-Hispanic whites (75 percent) are less likely to be caught in a squeeze between generations. They are most likely to live only with a spouse, without children or parents in the house, and they are more optimistic than other ethnic groups.

AARP announced that it will build on the survey's unique look at the sandwich generation from a multicultural perspective and already has established a dialogue with a number of interested organizations.

In responding to the survey, AARP pointed to several approaches that would address the challenges of the caregiver:

- Working individuals need more workplace flexibility to meet family caregiving demands. Such new practices should be supplementary to those included in the Family and Medical Leave Act, which was strongly endorsed by AARP.

- Prescription drug coverage in Medicare and the strengthening of Social Security are the twin centerpieces of AARP's advocacy program that would help ease the burden of caregiving.

- Caregiver programs should address the needs of diverse populations engaged in family caregiving through techniques such as multilingual staff and through programs that incorporate ethnic cultural traditions.

- The fragmented nature of home and community-based services for people in need of long-term care should be strengthened. Included would be improved financing, community-based navigation help for families, and greater coordination of service delivery to ensure that services are provided at the appropriate level. AARP is working to address these issues as well.

"Social and government institutions need to find ways to provide caregiver support to sandwich generation families, especially with life expectancy continuing to increase," said Novelli. "This is particularly true for minority and ethnic groups," he added.

Make Room for Granddaddy[6]

By Pamela Paul
American Demographics, April 2002

A typical Baby Boomer approaches each new life stage—parenting, empty-nesting or retirement—with zeal, interest and the intention to spend money. Allan Zullo of Asheville, N.C., was no exception. In 1996, when the then 47-year-old Zullo learned he was a grandfather-to-be, he immediately ran to the bookstore to get more information on his impending new role. What he found was "strictly geared to that gray-haired granny," not the energetic, young, still-working-full-time man he regarded himself to be. So Zullo and his wife Kathryn, then age 46, decided to write their own how-to book. The idea: to show just how different this new generation of grandparents is. "We're redefining the image of grandparents from the cookie-baking type to active grandparents who are in-line skating with their grandchildren," Zullo explains. "Today's grandparents are vibrant, alive, wear spandex and do yoga. We're very proactive in wanting to be part of our grandchildren's lives."

Say goodbye to the image of gray-haired grandparents in rocking chairs. As Baby Boomers enter this new life stage, they are adding their own twist to the idea of grandparenting. This new generation of grandparents is more youthful, more involved and has more money with which to dote on their grandkids. Today, a record 70 million Americans—about one-third of all adults—are grandparents, and the number is expected to rise to 80 million by 2010, according to Washington, D.C.-based AARP. The average age of a first-time grandparent today is 47—the average life expectancy just a century ago. With today's life expectancy of 76, this generation of elders may have as much as 30 years of grandparenting ahead of them.

What's more, they constitute a new market for businesses to tap: With grandparents spending an average of $500 a year on their grandchildren, up from $320 in 1992, grandparents constitute an annual $35 billion market. As Boomers—the 78 million Americans between the ages of 38 and 56—enter their prime grandparenting years, this market is bound to grow even larger.

Of course, grandparents have always spent money on their grandchildren. But how this particular generation of grandparents indulges its grandkids is likely to change, marketing experts say. There will be a new emphasis on services with an educational or instructional value, and long-term financial planning for a grand-

---

child's education and early adulthood. Already, more than half of grandparents (52 percent) help pay for their grandchildren's education, according to a 2002 AARP nationwide survey of 800 grandparents over the age of 50. Forty-five percent help pay for living expenses and 25 percent contribute to their grandchild's dental or medical costs. Vern Bengtson, a professor of gerontology and sociology at the University of Southern California, found that among his 150 students, 1 in 5 said their grandparents were paying all or part of their tuition.

Yet despite grandparents' formidable spending power, many experts say the grandparent market remains largely underserved. "This is a profoundly untapped market," says Ken Dychtwald, president and CEO of San Francisco-based consultancy Age Wave and author of *Age Power: How the 21st Century Will Be Ruled by the New Old* (Penguin/Tarcher, 2000). One reason why, according to Dychtwald, is that outdated images of grandparents cause many marketing messages to misfire. For example, although grandparents, and older people in general, are often perceived as frugal, Dychtwald says this idea actually stems from the preceding wave of grandparents, who grew up during the Depression and World War II. In contrast, this new generation of grandparents—Boomers—are not only among the wealthiest and most privileged segment of society, but they also tend to be proud of their largesse.

Last year, to better understand and predict this group's consumer behavior, SRI Consulting, a Menlo Park, Calif.-based marketing services firm, started to segment the grandparent population. SRI

Buy Me That!

Most grandparents (87 percent) are buying clothes for their grandchildren this year.

Items Purchased for Grandchildren Within the Past 12 Months:

	1999	2002
Clothing	74%	87%
Books	60%	80%
Fun food/snack food/fast food	n/a	78%
Educational toys (not for computer)	29%	n/a
Any other toys	38%	76%
Magazines	23%	32%
Music, CDs, tapes	n/a	48%
Videos, DVDs	n/a	45%
Jewelry	n/a	37%
Video games	n/a	31%
Computer software	18%	28%
Other electronic devices (radios, CD players)	n/a	28%
Tuition/day care	12%	n/a
Camp	11%	n/a

Source: AARP

coined three behavior categories to describe most grandparents. The first, "traditionalists," tend to be cautious, moralistic and patriotic, and account for the largest group of today's grandparents (54 percent), but is on the wane. As consumers, traditionalists are home-oriented, and prefer tried-and-true brands. The second group, "makers," (15 percent) is much more active than the first group, and is more likely to be independent and anti-authority. The third group, "achievers," (9 percent) is more status-oriented. They value interpersonal relationships and their buying behavior often relies on peer influence.

As Boomers start entering grandparenthood in droves, SRI sees a fourth group on the rise—"thinkers." Currently 16 percent of the grandparent population, they are more intellectually curious, active and globally oriented, and will start to replace the other three groups as Baby Boomers begin to dominate the grandparent population. This new group is driven by principles and doing what's right. They like to acquire information and are thoughtful in their purchasing behavior. They research products before buying them.

"The primary difference with the new wave of grandparents is they'll have a lot more resources—not just education and money, but also self-confidence, intellectualism and global awareness—that will make them more open-minded and expressive in the marketplace," says SRI senior consultant Kathy Whitehouse. Whereas in the past a grandparent might buy a toy based on functionality or durability, she says that the new grandparent will research the comparative merits of a toy and make a purchase based on its educational value, environmental quality and ability to engage.

Such changes are likely to be even more pronounced with the next wave of grandmothers—which includes the first generation of Boomer women to have their own careers. Women coming of grandmother age are more likely to be college-educated, to be employed outside the home, divorced or remarried and to have a sense of themselves as independent agents, according to Jean Giles-Sims, a sociologist at Texas Christian University and the founder of *www.grammystories.com*. Given the fact that grandparents are disproportionately female because of the higher mortality rate for men, such changes are significant. Giles-Sims is working on a new book, *Becoming Grammy: Today's Grandmothers Redefining the Old Stereotypes*, to address the impact of this transformation. "I call them 'empowered,'" she says. "And they've got much more money."

Take JoAnn Miller, a 64-year-old book editor in New York, and grandmother of three. Miller says the big difference between her generation and previous ones is that "we've got lives of our own." Miller, who spends about $4,000 a year on her grandchildren, says that her full-time job means that she's "not necessarily available to baby-sit."

Grandma, I'm Home!

A growing number of households are multigenerational, including grandparents, their children and grandchildren.

More grandparents are living with their grandchildren in multigenerational household settings. According to the Census Bureau, as of 2000, there were a total of 3.9 million multigenerational households in the U.S., making up 3.7 percent of the total population. Some 65 percent of those households consist of grandparents, their child or children and grandchildren. The remainder are households in which the middle generation acts as the head of household or the grandchild's generation serves as the head of household. "Grandparents today are more likely to deal with blended families. We're more likely to have parents who are still alive, so we've got four generations to contend with. And we're still working," says author Allan Zullo, who became a grandfather in his 40s.

States with a comparatively large percentage of multigenerational households include Hawaii, where 8.2 percent of all households are multigenerational. Puerto Rico also has a high rate (7.4 percent), particularly when compared with states such as North Dakota, where multigenerational households account for about 1 percent of the total number of households. Multigenerational households are also more likely to exist in areas heavily populated by new immigrants, areas with high out-of-wedlock birth rates where women often live with their parent(s) and areas with housing shortages or high living costs, according to demographer Lynne Casper, author of *Continuity and Change in the American Family* (Sage Publications, 2002).

The number of households maintained by a grandparent has also grown dramatically—to 3.9 million in 1998, from 2.2 million in 1970, an increase of 76 percent in 28 years. In a 1999 AARP national survey of 800 grandparents over age 50, 11 percent of grandparents identified themselves as caregivers, with 8 percent providing day care on a regular basis and 3 percent raising a grandchild by themselves.

According to a 1998 analysis by the Census Bureau, there are five main types of grandparent-maintained households: with both grandparents, and one or both parents present (34 percent of the total); both grandparents, no parents present (17 percent); grandmother only, some parents present (29 percent); grandmother only (14 percent); and grandfather only (6 percent). While the growth in the number of families with one parent and both grandparents present dominated the 1980s, since 1990, the most significant growth has been in households consisting of grandchildren and grandparents only, with neither parent present.

Certain characteristics apply to grandparent-headed households. As of 1997, half of the children living with grandparents were under age 6. Grandchildren living with their grandmothers tend to be black and live in urban centers. More than one-fourth of grandparent-raised (with either or both grandparents) children (27 percent) live in poverty; 63 percent of those living with a grandmother alone are impoverished. Grandparents raising their grandchildren are more likely to work: 72 percent of grandfathers and 56 percent of grandmothers are employed, compared with 33 percent and 24 percent respectively in parent-maintained homes.

A host of possible reasons can account for the increase in both multigenerational households and households in which the grandparents act as primary caregivers. The census report cites drug abuse among parents, teen pregnancy, divorce, the rise of single-parent households, mental and physical illness, AIDS, child abuse and imprisonment as the leading causes. Vern Bengtson, professor of gerontology and sociology at the University of Southern California, also attributes this growth to new laws on child endangerment, which have removed children from abusive-parent homes. He says there are pluses to these multigenerational households. "Multigenerational families are becoming more important for social support," he says. "And grandchildren are also increasingly taking care of both their grandparents and great-grandparents."

—Pamela Paul

Even grandmothers who don't work are different from previous generations, according to Giles-Sims. They're more active in their community, they travel, they volunteer. Many women between the ages of 40 and 65 approach grandparenting intent on making up for the mistakes they made with their own children during the 1970s. They see this as an opportunity to do things differently, she says.

Sara Schotland, 53, an attorney in Washington, D.C., says that her career path short-changed her on the full experience of parenting, so she was especially excited about the birth of her first granddaughter last year. She views grandparenting as "an opportunity to devote more time than I had as a parent." A third-year law student when she had her own daughter, and a young associate by the time she had her son, Schotland devotes time to her grandchildren that she didn't have for her children.

"I would never leave the office except in an emergency," she says. "But today, even though I'm still an active partner in my firm, the priority, time and attention for my granddaughter is without limit. I've left the office at 3 P.M. at least 10 times this year to tend to her needs."

High-Gear Grannies

Whether today's grandparents are more active or they just feel they have strength in numbers, the number of nanas and papas who engage in many activities that are not thought of as the "typical" for grandparents has more than doubled in the past 13 years. Specifically, New York City-based market research firm Mediamark Research, Inc. (MRI) reports that the number of grandparents of children under age 18 in the U.S. who play video games rose 208 percent between 1988 and 2001, the number who do aerobics grew 126 percent during the same time. Meanwhile, the number of grandparents who collect stamps, play cards and refinish furniture has risen at a much slower rate.

Activity done in the past year:	Grandparents (in millions)		Percent Increase
	1988	2001	
Weightlift	603	2,462	308%
Attend music and dance performances	3,271	10,703	227%
Play basketball	605	1,967	225%
Play video games	1,083	3,330	208%
Backpack/hike	744	1,904	156%
Aerobic exercise	1,472	3,323	126%
Collect stamps	1,344	1,999	49%
Play cards	9,782	12,009	23%
Refinish furniture	1,982	2,237	13%
Go on a picnic	6,457	6,725	4%

Source: Mediamark Research, Inc. (MRI) 1988, 2001

Indeed, grandparents today tend to be deeply involved in their grandkids' lives. According to a November 2001 AARP national survey of 823 grandparents over the age of 50, 78 percent have seen a grandchild in the past month or talked with them over the phone—and 65 percent say they speak at least once a week, up from 45 percent in a similar 1999 poll. In both surveys, approximately 85 percent said they shared a meal with their grandchild during the past six months; an equal number purchased their grandchild a gift; and more than half (53 percent) sent a greeting card in the past 30 days. Only 12 percent said they see or talk on the phone with their grandchildren every few months or less.

Summer Kircher will fly practically anywhere for her grandchildren. A 55-year-old part-time garden designer from Colorado Springs, Colo., the grandmother of three (with a fourth on the way) drives 70 miles to Denver every week to see her granddaughter and last year flew to Iowa six times to visit her son's two boys. Recently, Kircher even took one grandchild to Italy. "I'm not a baby-sitter," Kircher stresses. "I like to do things with them. I envision our activities as becoming even more experiential as they get older."

Grandfathers are no less involved than grandmothers. According to Bengtson at the University of Southern California, grandparenting is becoming much more important to American males. As men retire and live longer, Bengtson says, they're discovering not only their own children, but their grandchildren.

Whereas spending time together once revolved around home visits, today, multigenerational groups are more likely to go to a sporting event, take an educational day trip or participate in a physical

---

Dr. Spock for Grandparents

More than half (55 percent) of grandparents want more information on financing their grandchild's education.

Percent of Grandparents Who Say Information on the Following Topics Would be Useful:

	Very Useful	Somewhat Useful
Safety tips	34%	27%
Selecting age-appropriate books	32%	27%
Understanding teaching methods	33%	25%
Financing grandchild's education	29%	26%
Setting up savings or investments	27%	28%
Talking about sensitive topics	17%	37%
How to send email	24%	16%

Source: AARP, 1999

activity. Boomer grandparents are often looking for the same kinds of experiences they have sought throughout their lives: They want structured activities and organized events.

"We found that grandparents, especially Boomers, rather than buy things for their grandkids to do on their own, want to buy them experiences that they can do together," says Zullo, co-author of *The Nanas and the Papas: A Boomers' Guide to Grandparenting* (Andrews McNeel, 1998). "They want to travel together, go to camp together."

To be sure, not all of today's grandparents conform to this new portrayal of grandparenting. Experts hastily point out that the grandparent population is still diverse. Many grandparents continue to follow the traditional model. In addition to the larger shift towards more engaged grandparenting, Giles-Sims has uncovered a simultaneous smaller trend towards more remote grandparenting, cut off either by distance or conflict with children.

Charles Schewe, a principal of Lifestage Matrix, a Lafayette, Calif.-based market research firm and author of *Defining Markets-Defining Moments* (Hungry Minds Press, 2002), says the impact of Boomers will veer in a totally different direction. According to Schewe, the new Boomer grandparents will infuse their "Me Generation" mentality onto their grandchildren. "They'll be the distant grandparents," Schewe says. While they will still spend money, Schewe believes "they'll feel a desire to care for their grandchildren, but won't want to spend the energy and effort necessary to be a nurturing grandparent."

Yet the growth of this market seems not only certain, but set to accelerate as America becomes increasingly multigenerational. As lifespans continue to lengthen—and the definition of family takes on expanded meaning—we are likely to see households of up to

---

Grandma and Grandpa

They have on average five grandchildren and great-grandchildren.

Their Work Lives
56% are retired
23% work full time
8% work part time
7% are homemakers
30% have incomes of $50K plus

Their Grandchildren
58% have grandchildren age 3 or younger
57% have grandchildren ages 4–7
24% have great-grandchildren ages 4–7
59% have grandchildren ages 8–12
24% have a step-grandchild

Source: AARP, 1999

four generations. Of 823 respondents to a 2002 AARP survey, one-fourth of those polled also had great-grandchildren. According to Bengtson, in the past 30 years, there has been a ten-fold increase in the number of great-grandparents who are actively involved in the lives of their adolescent and young adult great-grandchildren.

"You're going to see a huge multiplication of the numbers of great-grandparents," says Dychtwald, who cites the growth of people becoming great-grandparents by the age of 60. Looks like we'll see greater grandparents in more ways than one.

II. The Collective Majority

Editor's Introduction

Although white people remain the racial majority in the United States, the 2000 Census reveals that minority groups are growing. With different cultural traditions and historical backgrounds, families belonging to these groups may vary enormously from the average white family, from other racial groups, and from subgroups within their own racial classification. The importance of family to the three largest minority groups in the United States—African Americans, Hispanic Americans, and Asian Americans—is examined in this section.

The alternative family structures in the African American community are the subject of Valerie Wilson Wesley's "Kindred." The author describes how the development of familial relationships was affected by slavery, in which one's family could be taken away at a moment's notice, prompting other members of the community to step in for those missing members. She points out that extended families are still an integral part of the black community and continue to shape the views of African Americans towards family.

"Time to Take a Closer Look at Hispanic Children and Families," a report authored by Kristin Anderson Moore, exposes some little-known facts about the growing Hispanic population in the United States. Statistics reveal that Hispanics—now the largest minority group in the nation—lag behind whites and blacks in education and health, have more children born to unwed or teenage mothers, and have higher rates of poverty and teenage suicide, but they tend to have healthier babies than the other two groups. The article points out the vast differences among those labeled Hispanic, a group encompassing dozens of nationalities and various language skills, from those who are native English speakers to bilingual individuals and those who speak only Spanish.

Finally, in "Culture Clash: Asian-American Families Struggle to Reconcile Expectations of East and West," Maria T. Padilla discusses the difficulties that arise when the children of Asian immigrants begin to assert their independence, often in their teenage years. These young people face the incompatible expectations of respecting the strict traditions of the old country while being accepted by their American peers. Padilla describes the tensions created by these expectations and by some parents' reluctance to relinquish control of their children's lives.

Kindred

A Portrait of Our Families Today[1]

By Valerie Wilson Wesley
Essence, December 1999

Reverence for kin is one of the strengths we brought with us from
the Motherland; it is one of those ancient Africanisms that still
sustain us. People of African descent have not only nurtured family
ties in the face of constant challenges to them, but have even pioneered new family forms to support us through whatever changing
and often harsh circumstances we find ourselves in. Throughout
our history we have recreated family the way we do our music,
style and food—by taking the little left us and claiming it, making
it our own and healing it with our particular brand of grace. We
shook up the institution of family and made it work for us, shaping
it to our lives. As a result, our families thrive in many diverse
forms as we move into the twenty-first century. In the following
pages, we represent the vitality and resilience of our people in a
contemporary family album.

Three centuries of slavery once taught us that our loved ones
didn't belong to us. Without warning, a mother could disappear forever; a child could be snatched or sold, leaving behind nothing but
a remembered smile or a lock of hair. So we learned to hold close
those who were with us, while clutching the memories of those who
were gone. And when freedom came, the first thing we did was
search for lost kin through newspaper ads, by word of mouth, on
foot when we could make it.

We forged kinship ties through necessity, and our extended families have always tended to expand rather than contract. We use
family terms inclusively. Cousins are simply cousins, be they first,
second or third (we rarely make those distinctions). Some historical research suggests that in the early days of slavery, *aunt* and
uncle were terms used to address the shipmates of an enslaved
child's parents, and later the terms were used to show respect to
elders. To this day, children call close friends of their parents aunt
and uncle.

A child born out of wedlock is not "illegitimate" in the eyes of our
community. We have never used legal terms to define the worth of
a child. Our children are our children.

---

1. Article by Valerie Wilson Wesley from *Essence* December 1999. Copyright © Valerie
Wilson Wesley. Reprinted with permission.

Many of us recognized early on the limitations inherent in a patriarchal family system that restricted both men and women. We adapted by evolving our own family systems—inclusive, sustaining, resourceful—ones that worked for us, protected our children, helped us survive. There were many hands tugging on the bootstrap that pulled us out of poverty. In this century during the Great Migration, clusters of kin and their close friends crowded into the same impoverished neighborhoods sharing what they had, protecting one another and one another's children in hostile cities. Our fathers nurtured. Our mothers worked. Our children pitched in. Our elders filled in. Our extended families—aunts, uncles, cousins, sisterfriends—watched our children and our backs.

So our families survive despite continuing reports of their demise. But even in this most prosperous of times, we remain disproportionately financially poorer than White families. The latest census figures show that close to 27 percent of our families make less than $15,000 a year compared with only 9 percent of White families. Twenty-four percent of Black families live below the 1997 poverty level of $16,400 in annual income for a family of four. Half of our children are raised in households headed by their mothers, compared with less than 20 percent of White children. Of those children being raised by women, half live in poverty. Among our elders, 26 percent are living below the poverty level, as compared with less than 10 percent of White seniors. Black men and White men have similar rates of raising their children without a partner, but the average income of Black-male single parents is far lower than that of their White counterparts.

Our families can certainly do better, but we've also done worse; there are some points of light within otherwise disheartening statistics. Census data show more than a third of our children have both parents in the home, and within these families, 29 percent earn from $30,000 to $49,999, and 44 percent earn at least $50,000. In terms of dollars, we're doing better than we've ever done. In 1967, only 10 percent of Black families earned $50,000 or more in today's dollars. By 1997, more than a quarter of all Black households earned at least $50,000.

1976	1990	1999
Alex Haley publishes *Roots*, the story of his own African-American family; the 1977 TV miniseries is the most watched of all time. Our families gain a new interest in genealogy.	The 1990 U.S. Census tallies that 42 percent of Black adults are married, down from 55 percent in 1970 and 63 percent in 1950.	Ghana, hosting the Fifth African–African-American Summit, announces legislation pending to allow foreigners applying for Ghanaian citizenship to hold dual nationalities.

As our families earn more money, more of us reach back to children who need help. That, too, is in our tradition. Although it is rarely acknowledged, African-American families adopt children at a higher rate than White families. Since the founding of adoption agencies that focus on the needs of Black children, the adoption rates of children by single Black parents have also increased. The great majority of children born to unmarried mothers and not cared for by them are raised by members of their extended families, often their grandmothers. The extended family continues to be the rock on which Black families stand. That rock occasionally rolls, often shifts, and sometimes even chips, but its indestructible core remains.

> *The extended family continues to be the rock on which Black families stand.*

And families continue to form where no blood ties exist. Historically, Black children were taken in by friends or caring members of the community when they needed to be rescued from a threatening situation or a situation where there was nobody to look after or raise them. Traditionally, the motherless child in the Black community has always found sympathy. Somebody looked out. Somebody stepped in. Somebody cared. It's a tradition we must continue.

We are pioneers when it comes to forming families. We merge, combine, stretch and create. Many different faces with different histories smile from the pages of our family albums.

Demographers have been predicting that the United States will become more multiracial in the twenty first century, but African-Americans have understood better than Whites the longstanding multiracial character of our families dating from slavery. Generations of White slaveowners sired mixed-raced offspring by Black women, never acknowledging these children and assigning them a marginal racial identity on the basis of one drop of African blood. Still, their Black families embraced them. Today, while it's true that the interracial marriage rates for Blacks have been increasing since 1960, we marry outside our racial group at far lower rates than Hispanics, Asians and Native Americans. We also have a long history of mixed bloodlines with other people of color in this hemisphere, but, paradoxically, when African-Americans marry outside our racial group, we most often marry Whites.

Our children represent our bond with the past and our link to the future. We will sustain and re-create our families in as many different ways as it takes to survive in this new millennium. We always have, we always will.

Family Profiles

By Amy DuBois Barnett

Modern Ghana's First Family

When Nana Konadu Agyeman first met Jerry John Rawlings, she was struck by his "very deep sense of justice." Well, that *and* his "rugged behavior"—to this day he enjoys scuba diving, skydiving and riding motorcycles. Once they wed in 1977, their lives quickly became embroiled in Ghana's. In 1979, young Flight Lieutenant Rawlings galvanized a coup against a corrupt military leadership and helped restore civilian rule and spur economic growth. In 1992, he became president in the nation's first multiparty democratic election. Today this beautiful coastal country is West Africa's most stable and prosperous nation.

The Rawlingses "try very hard to live a normal life," says the First Lady. The two youngest children, son Kimathi and daughter Amina, attend a local school; eldest daughter Zanetor is in medical school in Ghana. The second Rawlings daughter, Yaa Asantewaa, studies political science in England. President Rawlings, proud of all his children, has passed on to them his legacy of justice for all, often reminding them, "Power is only meaningful if it allows you to do positive things for the powerless."

It Takes a Village . . .

Most people would have thought that Ronnie and Karen Galvin had it made when they married in 1995. Still in their twenties, both were climbing that proverbial ladder of success in Atlanta: he was an account manager for a textiles firm; she was a corporate lawyer. But each felt a void. "We had very little time for each other or the community," says Karen. So she quit her fast-track job to fulfill a dream of becoming a juvenile-court judge. She further encouraged Ronnie, who was unenthusiastically contemplating returning to school for an M.B.A., to follow another road. Now in his final year of divinity school at Emory University, Ronnie has never been happier—not only because of his new vocation but also because of his growing family.

As a juvenile-court judge, Karen had been haunted by the many troubled children in foster care. And so, the Galvins adopted their son in 1998. When 15-month-old Darren joined his doting new parents, their entire Atlanta neighborhood celebrated the activist couple with a baby shower. Says Karen, "Darren has only added new dimensions to our love." Of his wife Ronnie says simply, "She has an incredible spirit."

The Blended Adams Family

Twelve years ago Derick Adams and Tanya Washington, both in first marriages, were coworkers at a Michigan bank; they became good friends. Five years later Derick's marriage broke up, then Tanya's. The two drew closer together, and Tanya's children, Micheal and Danielle, also became part of Derick's life. His daughter, Erin (who lives with her mother in Rochester, New York), would join the crew on frequent visits, completing this very nineties blended family.

In 1993, Derick got a great job offer in Boston, so he and Tanya got married and moved their joint household. But their time in Boston lasted only six months: Tanya and Derick profoundly missed their family and church network back in Michigan—all the more so once Tanya learned she was pregnant. So they moved back. Surprisingly, the kids were fine through the transitions. Says Derick, "It's because they all feel like they're getting attention and love. They don't have to compete for it." Tanya adds, "My children respect Derick, and Erin respects me. [My kids] call both Derick and my former husband Daddy."

All Together Now

When Karen Winston was 21 years old and her sister Barbara Pope was 19, the two got their first apartment together in New York City. They agreed that Barbara would help raise Karen's son, Tarik (now 24), and complete her college degree, while Karen worked and supported them all. After 25 years, they're still together, with some additions. Their young nephew, Sven, came to live with them first, then their baby sister, Zurn. (Their mother, Zurn Martina Porter, died unexpectedly two years ago at age 65.) Then their grandmother Katherine joined them in 1997, completing their tribe. The family now lives in a five-story Harlem brownstone that Barbara and Karen bought in 1998. Each floor has a separate apartment, but the ground floor is a common family area, and the doors to each unit are always open, giving this extended family the feeling of one big house. But living as several generations under one roof does take some effort. "We're all individuals who've learned tolerance and patience with each other," says Barbara. Karen adds, "There's a thread of true love that runs in this family."

Two Mommies, Two Sons

For April McLemore, the decision to move her children, Rashaad, 11, and Tariq, 6, from Atlanta, to the small town of Kyle, Texas, two and a half years ago was relatively easy—even though her friends thought she was nuts. After almost nine months of daily E-mails, huge telephone bills, and visiting back and forth, April relocated to be with her true love—Devetta Johnson, a Kyle resident who had responded to April's personal ad on America Online. "It was something I just felt," explains April, who in 1995 acknowledged that she was gay and ended her relationship with her boyfriend, who was her sons' father. The adjustment was rocky at first, with Devetta having to get used to an instant family, and the eldest boy missing his father so badly between visits to Atlanta that April found him a male mentor back in Kyle. But they're a tight family now. As for the kids' adjustment to their "two mommies"—when April asked Rashaad what he thought a lesbian was, he simply replied, "It's when two women live together and love each other and get along."

Bachelor Father

Though his friends were in shock at Randy Richardson's decision to take custody of his infant son, Romen, Randy saw it as a part of his plan. "When I was growing up, that's what I wanted . . . just me and a son," he says. "Now that I'm here, it's tough work." But Randy has lots of help: His mother and father, grandmother and great-grandmother all live on the same street he does. "Romen has three generations teaching him how to be a man," says Randy with a chuckle. Romen's mother, Tawnya Paolilli, 27, is also, as Randy puts it, his partner in parenting.

Randy was training to be a Navy Seal in 1997, but when he heard that his girlfriend was pregnant, he moved back to Portland, Oregon, where she was living. A month after their son was born, the two parents agreed that Romen would live with Randy. Still, Tawnya visits her son at Randy's house every day. Randy's long-term plans? "I hope that I'm lucky enough to get married one day, and that Romen can have some siblings," he says. But now his first priority is Romen: "Taking care of him is my main source of joy."

Honor-Roll Mom

What did 16-year-old honor-roll student LaTisha Price do between her sophomore and junior years of high school? She gave birth to a baby boy, Tarik, and learned how to take care of him. "At first I was kind of upset," LaTisha says about her pregnancy; she was five and a half months along before she realized it. But with the support of her mother, Gertrude Price, 53, with whom she and Tarik live, and help from Alan Rankin, her 17-year-old boyfriend and Tarik's father, LaTisha has adjusted to the demands of motherhood. "We just don't have that many problems," she says. "Alan and I really like to sit with the baby and make him laugh."

Still, having a baby before she turned sweet sixteen has profoundly changed her life. "I really don't do as much as I used to," says LaTisha. Though her situation isn't all that uncommon these days, her commitment to further her education is. After being home-tutored during the year she was pregnant, LaTisha eagerly returned to high school in September and diligently focuses on her academic program. After all, this dedicated and directed young mom wants to study computer science in college.

Rainbow Coalition

When Jeffrey first asked Theresa out—in their freshman year of high school—she declined because she didn't think he was serious. But two years later, when a mutual friend played matchmaker, they finally had their first date. They've been together ever since. Theresa's African-American family loved Jeffrey right away, and Jeffrey's Japanese-American mother welcomed Theresa. But Jeffrey's father, who was raised in Japan and retained traditional Japanese ideas of honoring ancestors and "pure" lineage, strongly objected. "No one who was not Japanese would have been acceptable," says Jeffrey. His father didn't attend Jeffrey and Theresa's wedding, but he came around after their son was born. He even took his grandson Derrik to Japan for a month to meet more of his Japanese relatives. "We taught the kids early on that it's not about what race you are, it's about who you are as a person," Theresa says about Derrik, 9, and daughter Serii, 5. Adds Jeffrey, "Our kids are the sum of two cultures. And they are very fortunate to have both."

Hip-Hop Newlyweds

Rap superstars Pepa and Treach first pledged to stay together for life earlier this year in Kansas City, getting wedding bands tattooed on their ring fingers. Then they did it again in a formal ceremony at their suburban New Jersey home on July 24. Pepa's son, Tyran, now calls Treach Daddy just like his little sister does. "Tyran used to be really jealous," recalls Treach. "He slowly started getting used to me and one day he asked me if I was his daddy, and I said yes."

Treach says he'll raise his kids not to expect the benjamins to flow without effort: "I don't want them to think that because mommy and daddy are famous, they can sit on their asses and not work hard. I want them to be in it to win it." Adds Pepa, "I want our kids to grow up with high self-esteem. It's important that they think, *I will do it and make it happen*, instead of *I can't*. Especially my daughter: You know—girl power!"

Time to Take a Closer Look at Hispanic Children and Families[2]

BY KRISTIN ANDERSON MOORE
POLICY & PRACTICE OF PUBLIC HUMAN SERVICES, JUNE 2001

The census results for the nation's Hispanic population seem to have taken many people by surprise. It's not that they did not expect the 2000 census to show growth in this population. They just did not expect that growth to be so large and to have occurred so swiftly—so fast that the numbers of Hispanics and African Americans in the nation are now just about equal.

What do we know about this booming population? For many Americans, the answer is, "Surprisingly little." They are aware that there are more Spanish-speaking people in their communities. But they do not know very much about what is going on in the lives of the Hispanic families they see and hear about.

At Child Trends, we track statistics on children and families. In the course of this work, we have noticed both warning flags and encouraging signs behind the explosive growth in the Hispanic population. What are some of the warning flags? Consider these measures of child and family well-being:

Education: Hispanics have lower high school completion rates than either whites or blacks, a trend that dates back to the early 1970s. The high school completion rate for Hispanics aged 18 to 24 in 1998 was only 63 percent, compared with 90 percent for whites and 81 percent for blacks.

Health: Hispanic children are less likely to have health insurance than either white or black children. In 1998, 70 percent of Hispanic children were covered by health insurance, compared with 96 percent of white and 80 percent of black children.

Family structure: Hispanic women now have the highest rate of out-of-wedlock births. In 1998, there were 90 out-of-wedlock births for every 1,000 unmarried Hispanic women aged 15 to 44. This rate was compared with 38 births for every 1,000 unmarried white women and 73 for every 1,000 unmarried black women.

Poverty: Hispanic children are more likely than either black or white children to be poor. They also are more likely to live in very poor neighborhoods, which often offer less social support to families raising children. In 1997, 61 percent of poor Hispanic children

---

2. Article by Kristin Anderson Moore from *Policy & Practice of Public Human Services* June 2001. Copyright © *Policy & Practice of Public Human Services*. Reprinted with permission.

lived in neighborhoods with a high concentration of poor residents (more than 40 percent in poverty), compared with 56 percent of poor white children and 53 percent of poor black children.

Teenage childbearing: Hispanic young women are more likely to become teenage parents than either their white or black counterparts. In 1996, the teenage birth rate was 177.8 for every 1,000 Hispanic females aged 15 to 19, compared with 68.1 per 1,000 for whites and 157.1 per 1,000 for blacks.

Youth suicide: Hispanic youth are more likely to report they have considered or attempted suicide. In 1999, 20 percent of Hispanic youth reported they had considered suicide, compared with 15 percent of black youth and 18 percent of white youth. Thirteen percent of Hispanic youth attempted suicide that year, compared with 7 percent of white and black youth.

In tracking the data on children, youth, and families, we also identified positive markers within the Hispanic population that warrant equal attention. For example, Hispanics outperformed blacks and whites on three measures of a healthy start to life. In 1998, Hispanics had:

- the lowest infant mortality rate (6 deaths per 1,000 live births, compared with 14 for blacks and 6 for whites);

- the lowest percentage of low-birth-weight babies (6 percent, compared with 13 percent for blacks and 7 percent for whites); and

- the lowest percentage of births to women who smoked during pregnancy (4 percent, compared with 10 percent for blacks and 16 percent for whites).

What's more, Hispanic women have made great strides in getting prenatal care. The percentage of Hispanic women receiving early prenatal care jumped from 60 percent in 1980 to 74 percent in 1998, reflecting similar improvements on this measure by white and black women.

This bad news/good news picture of conditions affecting Hispanic families and children is just one part of a larger picture of the Hispanic population at the beginning of this new century. It is a population that represents a rich mix of nationalities, embracing those with roots in Cuba, Mexico, Puerto Rico, Spain, and countries throughout Central and South America. It is a population that includes people whose families have lived in the United States for several generations and those who have just arrived. It is a population that includes those who struggle to read and write—in any language—as well as graduates of prestigious universities. With Hispanics, as with all ethnic groups, there is a profusion of variations.

Data can help us to identify and understand these variations. Most important, from a policy perspective, data can help us pinpoint where there are unmet needs within this large and diverse population so we can target our responses to these needs more effectively.

Take the statistics on high school completion rates. They suggest many Hispanic youth and young adults will be less prepared than their white and black peers to enter or progress in the labor force. Or, consider the statistics on youth suicide. They ought to raise questions about the causes of such despair and the availability of mental health or other services in Hispanic communities to combat it.

Consider the statistics on the teenage birth rate. They serve as a reminder of the need to couch campaigns to combat teenage pregnancy in language and action that is culturally sensitive, as well as to examine the special vulnerabilities in the lives of Hispanic youth. Or look at the statistics on health insurance coverage for Hispanic families. In the case of low-income families, they suggest many Hispanics are unaware of the availability of the Children's Health Insurance Program and other services for which they might be eligible.

For too long, we have cast social policy almost exclusively in terms of black-white relations. The Census 2000 numbers documenting the explosive growth of the Hispanic population are a wake-up call to widen our focus. And part of this involves paying attention—really paying attention—to the children and families behind the numbers.

Culture Clash

Asian-American Families Struggle to Reconcile Expectations of East and West[3]

By Maria T. Padilla
Orlando Sentinel, June 9, 1998

Marie Quiaoit was 19 before she had a steady boyfriend, and even then her parents weren't keen on the idea.

To help things go smoother, she offered to introduce her beau to her parents. But they nixed it.

"I don't think they liked the idea that I was dating, so they didn't want to meet the guy," says Ms. Quiaoit, now 24 and a student at the University of Central Florida. A similar scenario may be played out in many American homes, except at a younger age and perhaps with more negotiation on both sides.

Ms. Quiaoit is Philippine-born and American-raised, and that makes all the difference. Generational conflicts take on a different twist when the strict East meets the more liberal West.

Many Asian immigrant parents maintain Old World customs that permit their American offspring little wiggle room, and that generates cultural clashes.

Parental authority, honoring parents and conforming to family expectations are well-defined tenets in Asian cultures. In this country, challenging authority and staking one's independence are rewarded.

Now that immigration has made Asians the fastest-growing ethnic group in the country, these conflicts are the subject of many discussions and a few books.

"I think we're seeing a classic American pattern of assimilation, uneasy and fraught with tension but successful overall," says Frank Wu, a Chinese-American law professor in Washington, D.C., who writes frequently on Asian-American issues.

The Old World-to-New World transition has been characterized as "leaving deep water." In her book by the same name, author Claire S. Chow focuses on how the tensions affect Asian-American women.

"Those parents in some sense can't help what they do. Your instincts will be based on what you know," says Dr. Chow, a Chinese-American who practices marriage, family and child counseling in San Ramon, Calif.

That sometimes causes pain for the children, who are caught between two very different cultures.

---

3. Article by Maria T. Padilla from *Orlando Sentinel* June 9, 1998. Copyright © *Orlando Sentinel*. Reprinted with permission.

"You want to follow what your parents want you to do. But society is one way, and your parents have another way," Ms. Quiaiot says.

The issues most often revolve around dating, school and independence. The underlying theme seems to be personal freedoms.

"The children say, "We have our rights,'" says Sue Kiang, who lives in Orlando and has two children, ages 12 and 16.

"In America you have a lot of freedoms, the right to speak and express your thoughts. We are very conservative. We were brought up not to show off, to be humble," says Ms. Kiang, who was born in Hong Kong and raised in Phoenix.

As children enter their teens, they become more assertive. Relations can grow more tense, especially over dating.

"The monitoring of the socialization is a big issue for these families," says Rana Tiwari, originally of India.

Ms. Tiwari is a lawyer who recently moderated a discussion of similar issues at the University of Central Florida.

"You want to follow what your parents want you to do. But society is one way, and your parents have another way."—Marie Quiaiot, student.

Ms. Kiang would like her 16-year-old son to date a Chinese girl.

But the son responds, "What difference does it make? There are no Chinese girls at my school."

Kimiye Tipton, who is half-Japanese, recalls that she couldn't date until she was 17.

"I did everything very late," says Ms. Tipton, 44, who was raised in Arkansas and now lives in Winter Springs, Fla.

She says Asian cultural traditions can be a big burden for Asian-American children.

"There are huge traditions about how things are done. If you have a lot of tradition weighing you down, there's less and less speaking of your mind," Ms. Tipton says.

Ms. Tipton learned to hold her tongue when she visited relatives in Japan four years ago. She says she felt "shut down and muffled" as Japanese relatives explained how she ought to behave.

"I was being gathered into the fold, but it was a fold I was not comfortable in for more than a few weeks. I could be myself, but I felt constant pressure against it," says Ms. Tipton, who is married to a non-Asian and has a 10-year-old son.

The pressure to conform springs from the belief that children should not bring shame or dishonor on their family.

The feeling is so overwhelming that Dr. Chow, 45, was willing to edit passages in her book to which her mother might object.

Ms. Kiang says she would "never do anything against her parents' will."

And when her children started becoming more combative, she reminded them who was in charge of their home.

"I said, 'Don't you raise your voice at me. You have to show respect to your parents.' That's a written rule," Ms. Kiang says.

It's also "written" that children stay close to the family, which is different from the American belief that children should fly the coop. Cathy Wang of Longwood, Fla., says she lived with her parents until she was well into her career as a computer specialist.

"In the Asian community, you live with your parents until you're married," says Ms. Wang, who declined to give her age.

Taiwan-born Ms. Wang says the arrangement worked well for her.

"In the summer I had a small glass of freshly squeezed orange juice waiting for me in the fridge. In the winter, I had hot soup. I couldn't have asked for more," she says.

But many first- and second-generation Asian-Americans are asking for more—and getting it. Children are teaching their parents the art of negotiation, and this is making Asian families more "American."

For example, Ms. Wang's sister wanted to study music. But her parents, concerned about the sister's ability to earn a living, insisted on pharmacy. They worked out a compromise, allowing the sister to "try" pharmacy for one year. If she didn't like it, she could switch to music. In the end, music won out.

"The issue is not how the younger generation will react to parents, but how parents present the issue," Ms. Wang says.

Ms. Tiwari, the lawyer, has tried to raise her son to be a "sensitive guy of the '90s." Still, she insists that negotiation and compromise are necessary for parents and children.

"Total independence at the cost of others is not what it's about. Your independence has to be tempered by the needs of other people and the functionality of the group," Ms. Tiwari says.

University student Quiaiot, who lives at home, says relations have improved with her parents. However, they have some issues to resolve.

"I don't think they'll ever accept the fact that I'm going to be independent," she says.

III. Marriage and Other Partnerships

Editor's Introduction

The married couple has been the traditional cornerstone of the family, but like nearly everything else concerning American families, what was once taken for granted as a necessity has now become only one of many options. While marriage remains the ideal for the vast majority of Americans, divorce has become a common end to wedded unions. The high number of divorces has prompted some experts to seek ways to make ending a marriage more difficult, often citing the well-being of the children as a reason for remaining in a less than fulfilling partnership. Other couples choose not to marry at all, but live together many years with or without having children. Homosexual couples find this option is forced upon them by a legal system that does not recognize gay marriages. Section III considers various forms of marriage in America and how they are shaping conceptions of family.

"The State of Our Unions," written by David Popenoe and Barbara Dafoe Whitehead, is a statistical look at Americans' attitudes towards matrimony. While most young people still cherish the idea of remaining married to the same person their entire lives, the overall marriage rate has declined and the age at which men and women are first married has risen. The increased acceptance of living together outside of marriage or raising children while single are cited as contributing factors to these trends, as is the increased importance of having a career for women. The rise in the divorce rate reflects changes in *why* people marry, which is more likely to be prompted by a desire to find a soul mate than economic necessity or religious morality.

The *Time* magazine article "Should You Stay Together for the Kids?" explores the impact of divorce on children. Young people often cite their parents' divorce as a cause of shattered self-confidence and a lack of trust in others, effects that can be long-lasting and deeply felt. Although some experts assert that many of the problems these children face may have been present before their parents split up, others, like noted author Judith Wallerstein, have suggested that parents who are truly concerned about their children's welfare should consider staying in a bad marriage for their sake, a notion that has elicited fierce attacks from her critics.

The difficulties of dissolving a long-term same-sex relationship is the topic of Mubarak Dahir's "Breaking Up Is Hard to Do." With little socially or legally accepted recognition of the validity of their relationship, when a gay or lesbian couple breaks up, partners have a limited claim to the kind of financial support or child visitation rights available to heterosexual married couples who divorce, even if one member of the pair has been staying at home raising children. When such cases do end up in the courts, they are often treated as business arrangements, since there are few legal precedents for treating them as family disputes.

The State of Our Unions[1]

By David Popenoe and Barbara Dafoe Whitehead
USA Today Magazine, July 2002

Each year, the National Marriage Project at Rutgers University publishes an assessment of the health of marriage and marital relationships in America entitled "The State of Our Unions." It is based on a thorough review and evaluation of the latest statistics and research findings about marriage, family, and courtship trends, plus our own special surveys. For this year's report, we commissioned the Gallup Organization to do a national representative telephone survey of people in their 20s; 1,003 men and women were interviewed. The kinds of questions to which we sought answers included: Are young adults interested in getting married? What traits are they looking for in a marriage partner? How do their attitudes about marriage differ from those of their parents? Here are our findings:

Americans haven't given up on marriage as a cherished ideal. Indeed, most continue to prize and value it as an important life goal, and the vast majority (an estimated 85%) will marry at least once in a lifetime. Almost all couples enter marriage with a strong desire and determination for a life-long, loving partnership, and this desire may even be increasing among the young. Since the 1980s, the percentage of high school seniors who say that having a good marriage is extremely important to them as a life goal has gone up, though only slightly.

Nevertheless, in recent decades, Americans have become less likely to marry. This is indicated by a marriage-rate decline of more than one-third between 1970 and the mid 1990s. The number of marriages per 1,000 unmarried women 15 and over was 76.5 in 1970, dropping to 49.7 in 1996. This is due partly to the delaying of first marriages until older ages, as the median age at first marriage went from 20 for females and 23 for males in 1960 to about 25 and 27, respectively, today. Other factors accounting for the decline of the marriage rate are the growth of living together outside of marriage and small decreases in the tendency of people ever to marry and of divorced persons to remarry.

Moreover, when men and women do marry, they are entering a union that looks very different from the one that their parents or grandparents did. We have identified five areas in which major changes have occurred:

---

1. Article by David Popenoe and Barbara Dafoe Whitehead from *USA Today Magazine* July 2002. Copyright © SAE Inc. Reprinted with permission.

As a **couples relationship,** marriages today are more likely to be broken by divorce than by death. Americans may marry, but they have a hard time achieving successful marriages. Although the divorce rate has dropped slightly since the early 1980s, when it was close to 50% of all marriages, it remains between 40 and 45%.

Divorce has become a pervasive reality in the lives of today's young people, as well as an ever-present theme in the books, music, and movies of the youth culture. The specter of divorce is widespread, with more than half of the twentysomethings interviewed in our Gallup survey agreeing that "one sees so few good or happy marriages today that one questions it as a way of life." Among single young adults, the same percentage said that one of their biggest concerns about marriage is "the possibility that it will end in divorce."

As a **rite of passage,** marriage is losing much of its social importance and ritual significance. It is no longer the standard pathway from adolescence to adulthood for young adults. It is far less likely than in the past to be closely associated with the timing of the first sexual intercourse for young women, and less likely to be the first living together union for young couples. Over half of all first marriages today are preceded by unmarried cohabitation, compared to virtually none early in the 20th century. Young adults are postponing marriage until their middle to late 20s, and most women as well as men have established themselves in jobs and careers before they marry. They spend a long period as never-married, but sexually active, singles in a new stage of life we have described as one of "sex without strings, relationships without rings."

> *"One sees so few good or happy marriages today that one questions it as a way of life."*—Gallup survey.

As a **long-term childrearing partnership,** marriage has weakened dramatically. Only 16% of the young adults in our Gallup survey agreed that "the main purpose of marriage these days is to have children." In addition to the high divorce rate, which affects over 1,000,000 children each year, an additional one-third of all children today are born out of wedlock. There has also been an enormous increase in the number of unmarried cohabiting couples who live with children. As a consequence, 68% of all children are now living with two parents, compared to 85% as recently as 1970.

Most disquieting, with worrisome consequences for children, is young people's growing acceptance of unwed parenthood. In our survey, 62% of the men agreed that "while it may not be ideal, it's okay for an adult woman to have a child on her own if she has not found the right man to marry." We did not ask the women this question, but we know from other data that their response would have been similar. Indeed, it often seems that the larger society has pretty much surrendered to the notion that anything goes in family life as long as it doesn't hurt, tax, or impinge on the freedom of another adult individual.

As a **stage in the life course of adults,** marriage is shrinking. Americans are living longer, marrying later, exiting marriages more quickly, and choosing to live together before marriage, after marriage, in between marriages, and as an alternative to marriage. A small but growing percentage, an estimated 15%, will never marry, compared to about five percent during the 1950s. As a consequence, marriage gradually is giving way to partnered and unpartnered singlehood, with or without children. Since 1960, the percentage of persons age 35 through 44 who were married has dropped from 88% to 69% for men and 87% to 71% for women.

As an **institution,** marriage has lost much of its legal, social, economic, and religious meaning and authority. The marital relationship once consisted of an economic bond of mutual dependency, a social bond supported by the extended family and larger community, and a spiritual bond upheld by religious doctrine, observance, and faith. Today, there are many marriages that have none of these elements. The older ideal of marriage as a permanent contractual union, strongly supported by society and designed for procreation and childrearing, is giving way to a new reality of it as a purely individual contract between two adults. Moreover, marriage is also quietly losing its place in the language and in popular culture. Unmarried people now tend to speak inclusively about "relationships" and "intimate partners." In the entertainment industry—including films, television, and music—marriage is often neglected or discredited.

> *As an institution, marriage has lost much of its legal, social, economic, and religious meaning and authority.*

If these have been the main changes, what, then, has marriage become in 21st-century America? First, let us not forget that many of the marriage-related trends of recent decades have been positive. The legal, sexual, and financial emancipation of women has become a reality as never before in history. With few restrictions on divorce, a married woman who is seriously abused by her husband can get out of the relationship, which she previously might have been stuck in for life. Due to great tolerance of family diversity, adults and children who through no fault of their own end up in nontraditional families are not marked for life by social stigma. Moreover, based on a companionship of equals, many marriages today may be more emotionally satisfying than ever before.

We have described the new marriage system as "emotionally deep, but socially shallow." For most Americans, marriage is a "couples relationship" designed primarily to meet the sexual and emotional needs of the spouses. Increasingly, happiness in marriage is measured by each partner's sense of psychological well-being, rather than the more-traditional measures of getting ahead economically, boosting children up to a higher rung on the educational ladder than the parents, or following religious teachings on marriage. People tend to be puzzled or put off by the idea that marriage has purposes or benefits that extend beyond fulfilling individual adult needs for intimacy and satisfaction. Eight out of 10 of the young adults in our survey agreed that "marriage is nobody's business, but that of the two people involved."

It is a sign of the times that the overwhelming majority (94%) of never-married singles in our survey agreed that "when you marry, you want your spouse to be your soul mate, first and foremost." This perspective, surely encouraged not only by the changing nature of marriage, but by the concern about divorce and therefore the seeming necessity of finding the one right person, is something that most people in the older generation would probably consider surprising. In times past, people married to start a new family, and therefore they looked for a competent and reliable mate to share life's tasks. To the degree that a soul mate was even considered, it was more likely to have been thought of as the end result of a lifetime of effort put into making a marriage work, not something you start out with.

Of course, having a soul mate as a marriage partner would be wonderful. In many ways, it is reassuring that today's young people are looking for a marriage that is both meaningful and lasting. Yet, there is a danger that the soul mate expectation sets a standard so

---

There is a danger that the soul mate expectation sets a standard so high it will be hard to live up to.

---

high it will be hard to live up to. Also, if people believe that there is just one soul mate waiting somewhere out there for them, as most of today's youths in fact do according to our survey, doesn't it seem more likely that a marriage partner will be dropped when the going gets rough? Isn't it easier to say, "I must have picked the wrong person"? In other words, perhaps we have developed a standard for marriage that tends to destabilize the institution.

There are some hopeful signs in the recent statistics that may bode well for the future of marriage. The divorce rate has slowly been dropping since the early 1980s. Since the early 1990s, the teen birthrate has decreased by about 20%, with some indications that teenagers have become sexually more conservative. Overall, the percentage of unwed births has remained at its current level for the past five years. Indeed, due to fewer divorces and stabilized unwed births, the percentage of children living in single-parent families dropped slightly in the past few years, after having increased rapidly and continuously since 1960.

Moreover, one can see glimmers of hope here and there on the cultural scene. There are stirrings of a grassroots "marriage movement." Churches in several hundred communities have joined together to establish a common set of premarital counseling standards and practices for engaged couples. Marriage education has emerged as a prominent theme among some family therapists, family life educators, schoolteachers, and clergy. In several states, legislatures have passed bills promoting marriage education in the schools and even seeking ways to cut the divorce rate, mainly through educational means. More books are being published with the theme of how to have a good marriage, and seemingly fewer with the theme of divorcing to achieve personal liberation. Questions are being raised more forcefully by members of Congress, on both sides of the aisle, about the "family values" of the entertainment industry. These positive trends bear watching and are encouraging, but it is too soon to tell whether they will persist or result in the revitalization of this critical social institution.

Should You Stay Together for the Kids?[2]

BY WALTER KIRN
TIME, SEPTEMBER 25, 2000

One afternoon when Joanne was nine years old she came home
from school and noticed something missing. Her father's jewelry box
had disappeared from its usual spot on her parents' bureau. Worse,
her mother was still in bed. "Daddy's moved out," her mother told
her. Joanne panicked. She began to sob. And even though Joanne is
40 now, a married Los Angeles homemaker with children of her
own, she clearly remembers what she did next that day. Her vision
blurred by tears, she searched through the house that was suddenly
not a home for the jewelry box that wasn't there.

Time heals all wounds, they say. For children of divorce like
Joanne, though, time has a way of baring old wounds too. For
Joanne, the fears that her parents' split unleashed—of abandon-
ment, of loss, of coming home one day and noticing something missing from the bedroom—deepened as the years went by. Bursts of
bitterness, jealousy and doubt sent her into psychotherapy. "Before
I met my husband," she remembers, "I sabotaged all my other relationships with men because I assumed they would fail. There was
always something in the back of my head. The only way I can
describe it is a void, unfinished business that I couldn't get to."

For America's children of divorce—a million new ones every
year—unfinished business is a way of life. For adults, divorce is a
conclusion, but for children it's the beginning of uncertainty. Where
will I live? Will I see my friends again? Will my mom's new boyfriend leave her too? Going back to the early '70s—the years that
demographers mark as the beginning of a divorce boom that has
receded only slightly despite three decades of hand wringing and
worry—society has debated these children's predicament in much
the same way that angry parents do: by arguing over the little ones'
heads or quarreling out of earshot, behind closed doors. Whenever
concerned adults talk seriously about what's best for the children of
divorce, they seem to hold the discussion in a setting—a courtroom
or legislature or university—where young folks aren't allowed.

---

2. Copyright © 2000 TIME Inc. reprinted by permission.

That's changing. The children are grown now, and a number are speaking up, telling stories of pain that didn't go away the moment they turned 18 or even 40. A cluster of new books is fueling a backlash, not against divorce itself but against the notion that kids somehow coast through it. Stephanie Staal's *The Love They Lost* (Delacorte Press), written by a child of divorce, is part memoir and part generational survey, a melancholy volume about the search for love by kids who remember the loss of love too vividly. *The Case for Marriage* by Linda Waite and Maggie Gallagher (Doubleday) emphasizes the positive, arguing that even rocky marriages nourish children emotionally and practically.

The most controversial book, comes from Judith Wallerstein, 78, a therapist and retired lecturer at the University of California, Berkeley. In *The Unexpected Legacy of Divorce* (Hyperion) she argues that the harm caused by divorce is graver and longer lasting than we suspected. Her work raises a question that some folks felt was settled back in the days of *Love, American Style*: Should parents stay together for the kids?

> **By the Numbers: The State of Divorce Around the Globe**
>
> The U.S. is certainly not the divorce capital of the world.
>
> Divorces as a percent of all marriages:
> - Russia 65%
> - Sweden 64%
> - Finland 56%
> - Britain 53%
> - U.S. 49%
> - Canada 45%
> - France 43%
> - Germany 41%
> - Israel 26%
> - Greece 18%
> - Spain 17%
> - Italy 12%

Listening to children from broken families is Wallerstein's lifework. For nearly three decades, in her current book and two previous ones, she has compiled and reflected on the stories of 131 children of divorce. Based on lengthy, in-depth interviews, the stories are seldom happy. Some are tragic. Almost all of them are as moving as good fiction. There's the story of Paula, who as a girl told Wallerstein, "I'm going to find a new mommy," and as a young woman—too young, it turned out—impulsively married a man she hardly knew. There's Billy, born with a heart defect, whose parents parted coolly and amicably but failed to provide for his pressing medical needs.

It's the rare academic who can make a reader cry. Maybe that's why, with each new installment, Wallerstein's study has created shock waves, shaping public opinion and even the law. Her attention-getting style has proved divisive. For experts in the field of family studies (who tend to quarrel at least as bitterly as the dysfunctional clans they analyze), she's a polarizing figure. To her admirers, this mother of three and grandmother of five, who has been married to the same man for 53 years, is a brave, compassionate voice in the wilderness. To her detractors, she's a melodramatic doomsayer, a crank.

Children at Risk

Over 1 million children are involved in new divorces each year.

Percent of children under 18 living with only one parent:
- 1970 12%
- 1996 28%

Single-parent status:
- Divorced 37%
- Never married 36%
- Separated 23%
- Widowed 4%

What drew someone from such a stable background to the study of marital distress? At the end of the 1960s, Wallerstein, whose Ph.D. is in clinical psychology, moved from Topeka, Kans., in the ho-hum heartland, to swinging California. "Divorce was almost unheard of in the Midwest," she recalls. Not so on the Gold Coast, the state had just passed its pioneering no-fault divorce law. Wallerstein took a job consulting at a large community mental-health center in Marin County just as the social dam began to crack. "We started to get complaints," she says, "from nursery school teachers and parents: 'Our children are having a very hard time. What should we do?'"

The prevailing view at the time, she says, was that divorce was no big deal for kids. So much for the power of positive thinking. "We began to get all these questions," Wallerstein remembers. "The children were sleepless. The children in the nursery school were aggressive. They were out of control." When Wallerstein hit the library for answers, she discovered there were none. The research hardly existed, so she decided to do her own. She had a hunch about what she would learn. "I saw a lot of children very upset," she says, "but I fully expected that it would be fleeting."

Her hunch was wrong. Paradise for kids from ruptured families wasn't easily regained. Once cast out of the domestic garden, kids dreamed of getting back in. The result more often than not was frustration and anxiety. Children of divorce suffer depression, learning difficulties and other psychological problems more frequently than those of intact families. Some of Wallerstein's colleagues, not to mention countless divorced parents, felt they were being guilt-tripped by a square. They didn't want to hear this somber news.

Now, decades later, some still don't want to hear her. For parents, her book's chief finding, to be sure, is hardly upbeat or very reassuring: children take a long time to get over divorce. Indeed, its most harmful and profound effects tend to show up as the children reach maturity and struggle to form their own adult relationships. They're gun-shy. The slightest conflict sends them running. Expecting disaster, they create disaster. "They look for love in strange places," Wallerstein says. "They make terrible errors of judgment in whom they choose."

Marcie Schwalm, 26, a Bloomington, Ill., legal secretary whose parents split when she was four, illustrates Wallerstein's thesis well. As a young woman she couldn't seem to stick with the same boyfriend. "I thought guys were for dating and for breaking up with a few weeks later," she says. "I would go into a relationship wondering how it was going to end." Finally, Marcie says, a college beau told her she had a problem. She's married now, and her feelings about divorce have a hard-line, 1950s tone: "Divorce is not something I am going to go through. I would do whatever it takes to keep the marriage together."

Kristina Herrndobler, 17, isn't so sure that harmony can be willed. Now a high school student in Benton, Ill., she too was four when her parents called it quits. She says she has no memories of the trauma, just an abiding skepticism about marriage and a resolve to settle for nothing less than the ideal man. "I don't want my kids to wind up in a single-parent situation," she says. "And I don't want to have kids with a man I don't want to be married to forever. I don't believe in the fairy tale. I hope it exists, but I really don't believe it does."

And therein lies another problem, according to Wallerstein: the belief, quite common in children of divorce, that marriage is either a fairy tale or nothing. These jittery, idealistic children tend to hold out for the perfect mate—only to find they have a very long wait. Worse, once they're convinced they've found him, they're often let down. High romantic expectations tend to give way, Wallerstein reports, to bitter disillusionments. Children from broken families tend to marry later, yet divorce more often than those from intact homes.

So divorce often screws up kids. In itself, this isn't news, though many experts feel Wallerstein overstates the case. That divorce may screw them up for a long, long time and put them at risk for everything from drug abuse to a loveless, solitary old age is more disturbing—and even more debatable. Christy Buchanan, a professor of psychology at Wake Forest University and co-author of *Adolescents After Divorce* (Harvard), is typical of Wallerstein's detractors. "I think the main drawback of the sort of research she does is that you can't necessarily generalize it to a broad population," Buchanan says. "The other caution I would put forth is that

---

Divorce Data

- More than 40% of first marriages end in divorce.
- Total number of divorced adults grew from 4.3 million in 1970 to 20 million today.
- Married population dropped from 72% in 1970 to 60% today.
- Average duration of first marriages ending in divorce is eight years; duration of second marriages is six years.
- Average total household wealth of those ages 51 to 61:
  Married couples $132,000
  Divorced $33,700
  Widowed $42,300

she has a group of divorced families but no comparison group of non-divorced families. [Perhaps in response to this longstanding complaint, Wallerstein also interviewed children of intact marriages for her new book.] There's some good research suggesting that many of the problems that have been attributed to divorce in children were actually present prior to the divorce."

Not rigorous enough. Too gloomy. Those are the leading raps against Wallerstein. Paul Amato, a sociology professor at Penn State, has researched divorce and children for 20 years, casting the sort of wide statistical net that hardheaded academics favor and Wallerstein eschews as too impersonal. While Amato agrees with her about divorce's "sleeper effect" on children—the problems that crop up only after they're grown—he finds her work a bit of a bummer. "It's a dismal kind of picture that she paints," he says. "What most of the large-scale, more scientific research shows is that although growing up in a divorced family elevates the risk for certain kinds of problems, it by no means dooms children to having a terrible life."

And what about children raised from the start by single moms? Last month, *Time* ran a story about the challenges faced by single women having children of their own. But in all the coverage about how those women are coping, the impact on the kids is sometimes underplayed—and their issues are not that different from those of kids from divorced households. "Some studies have directly compared children who were raised by mothers who are continuously single with mothers who went through a divorce," says Amato. "In general, the outcomes for children seem to be pretty similar. It

---

TIME/CNN Poll

Do you agree or disagree that for the children's sake, parents should stay together and not get a divorce, even if the marriage isn't working?

	1981	2000
Agree parents should stay together	21%	33%
Disagree	71%	62%

Are children better off in:
• An unhappy marriage in which parents stay together mainly for kids? 23%
• A divorce in which the parents are more happy? 66%
• Not sure 11%

When parents get divorced, are children harmed?
• Almost always harmed 42%
• Frequently harmed 22%
• Sometimes harmed 27%
• Seldom harmed 8%

appears to increase the risk for some types of problems: in conduct, in school, in social relations. Neither one appears to be optimal for children."

Besides her conclusions on children's long-term prospects following divorce, Wallerstein makes another major point in her book—one that may result in talk-show fist-fights. Here it is: children don't need their parents to like each other. They don't even need them to be especially civil. They need

> *A lousy marriage, at least where the children's welfare is concerned, beats a great divorce.*

them to stay together, for better or worse. (Paging Dr. Laura!) This imperative comes with asterisks, of course, but fewer than one might think. Physical abuse, substance addiction and other severe pathologies cannot be tolerated in any home. Absent these, however, Wallerstein stands firm: a lousy marriage, at least where the children's welfare is concerned, beats a great divorce.

Them's Fighting Words

The shouting has already started. Family historian Stephanie Coontz, author of *The Way We Never Were: American Families and the Nostalgia Trap* (Basic) questions the value of papering over conflicts for the kids' sake. Sure, some parents can pull it off, but how many and for how long? "For many couples," Coontz says, "things only get worse and fester, and eventually, five years down the road, they end up getting divorced anyway, after years of contempt for each other and outside affairs."

Coontz doesn't believe in social time travel. She doesn't think we can go back to *Leave It to Beaver* after we've seen *Once and Again*. Unlike Wallerstein, whose investigation is deep but rather narrow (the families in her original study were all white, affluent residents of the same Northern California county, including non-working wives for whom divorce meant a huge upheaval), Coontz takes a lofty, long view of divorce. "In the 1940s the average marriage ended with the death of the spouse," Coontz says. "But life expectancy is greater today, and there is more potential for trouble in a marriage. We have to become comfortable with the complexity and ambiguity of every family situation and its own unique needs."

That's just a lot of fancy, high-flown talk to Wallerstein and her followers. Ambiguity doesn't put dinner on the table or drive the kids to soccer practice or save for their college education. Parents do. And parents tend to have trouble doing these things after they get divorced. In observing what goes wrong for kids when their folks decide to split, Wallerstein is nothing if not practical. It's not just the absence of positive role models that bothers her; it's the depleted bank accounts, the disrupted play-group schedules, the frozen dinners. Parents simply parent better, she's found, when there are two of them. Do kids want peace and harmony at home? Of course. Still, they'll settle for hot meals.

Wallerstein didn't always feel this way. Once upon a time, she too believed that a good divorce trumped a bad marriage where children were concerned. "The central paradigm now that is subscribed to throughout the country," says Wallerstein, "is if at the time of the breakup people will be civil with each other, if they can settle financial things fairly, and if the child is able to maintain contact with both parents, then the child is home free." Wallerstein helped build this model, she says, but now she's out to tear it down. "I'm changing my opinion," she says flatly.

The family-values crowd is pleased as punch with Wallerstein's change of heart. Take David Blankenhorn, president of the Institute for American Values. "There was a sense in the '70s especially, and even into the '80s, that the impact of divorce on children was like catching a cold: they would suffer for a while and then bounce back," he says. "More than anyone else in the country, Judith Wallerstein

---

Personal growth is a poor excuse for dragging the little ones through a custody battle that just might divide their vulnerable souls into two neat, separate halves doomed to spend decades trying to reunite.

---

has shown that that's not what happens." Fine, but does this oblige couples to muddle through misery so that Johnny won't fire up a joint someday or dump his girlfriend out of insecurity? Blankenhorn answers with the sort of certainty one expects from a man with his imposing title. "If the question is, 'If unhappily married parents stay together for the sake of their kids, will that decision benefit their children?' the answer is yes."

We can guess how the moral stalwarts will answer such questions. What about ordinary earthlings? Virginia Gafford, 56, a pet-product saleswoman in Pawleys Island, S.C., first married when she was 19. The marriage lasted three years. She married again, had a second child, Denyse, and divorced again. Denyse was 14. She developed the classic symptoms. Boyfriends jilted her for being too needy. She longed for the perfect man, who was nowhere to be found. "I had really high expectations," says Denyse. "I wanted Superman, so they wouldn't do what Dad had done." Denyse is in college now and getting fine grades, but her mother still has certain regrets. "If I could go back and find any way to save that marriage, I'd do it," she says. "And I'd tell anyone else to do the same."

For Wallerstein and her supporters, personal growth is a poor excuse for dragging the little ones through a custody battle that just might divide their vulnerable souls into two neat, separate halves

Is Divorce Getting a Bum Rap?

Are Americans a nation of frivolous divorcers who selfishly pursue the bluebird of happiness, oblivious to their children's needs? Divorce opponents like Judith Wallerstein seem to think most parents see divorce as a marvelous opportunity for the whole family. How immature do they think people are? All over America, unhappy spouses lie awake at night wondering if they and their kids can afford divorce—financially, socially, emotionally. Where will they live, how will they pay the bills, will the kids fall apart, will there be a custody battle, what will their families say? The very fact that so many people leave their marriage for a future with so many pitfalls proves that divorce is anything but a whim. Most people I know who split up (not to mention my ex and me) spent years working up to it.

In her new book, Wallerstein argues that children don't care if their parents are happy—they just want the stability of a two-parent household, without which they would later flail through adulthood and have a hard time forming good relationships. This conclusion, like her other gloomy generalizations ("Parenting erodes almost inevitably at the breakup and does not get restored for years, if ever"), is based on a small, nonrepresentative sample of families who were going through divorce in 1971 in affluent Marin County, Calif. Wallerstein looks for evidence that divorce harms kids, and of course she finds it—now well into their mid-30s, her interviewees still blame their parents' breakup for every rock on the path to fulfillment—but the very process of participating in a famous on-going study about the effects of divorce encourages them to see their lives through that lens. What if she had spent as much time studying children whose parents had terrible marriages but stayed together for the kids? How many 35-year-old "children" would be blaming their problems on the nights they hid in their rooms while Mom and Dad screamed at each other in the kitchen? Wallerstein points out that many children of divorce feel overly responsible for their parents' happiness. But what about the burden of knowing that one or both of your parents endured years of misery—for you?

As a matter of fact, we know the answer to that question. The baby boomers, who helped divorce become mainstream, were the products of exactly the kind of marriages the anti-divorcers approve of—the child-centered unions of the 1950s, when parents, especially Mom, sacrificed themselves on the altar of family values and suburban respectability. To today's anti-divorcers those may seem like "good enough" marriages—husband and wife rubbing along for the sake of the children. The kids who lived with the silence and contempt said no thank you.

America doesn't need more "good enough" marriages full of depressed and bitter people. Nor does it need more pundits blaming women for destroying "the family" with what are, after all, reasonable demands for equality and self-development. We need to acknowledge that there are lots of different ways to raise competent and well-adjusted children, which—as, according to virtually every family researcher who has worked with larger and more representative samples than Wallerstein's tiny handful—the vast majority of kids of divorce turn out to be. We've learned a lot about how to divorce since 1971. When Mom has enough money and Dad stays connected, when parents stay civil and don't bad-mouth each other, kids do all right. The "good enough" divorce—why isn't that ever the cover story?

doomed to spend decades trying to reunite. Anne Watson is a family-law attorney in Bozeman, Mont., and has served as an administrative judge in divorce cases. She opposes tightening divorce laws out of fear that the truly miserable—battered wives, the spouses of alcoholics—will lose a crucial escape route. But restless couples who merely need their space, in her opinion, had better think twice and think hard. "If people are divorcing just because of choices they want to make, I think it's pretty tough on the kids," Watson says. "Just because you're going to feel better, will they?"

That, of course, is the million-dollar question. Wallerstein's answer is no, they'll feel worse. They'll feel worse for quite a while, in fact, and may not know why until they find themselves in court, deciding where their own kids will spend Christmas. It's no wonder Wallerstein's critics find her depressing.

Does Wallerstein's work offer any hope or guidance to parents who are already divorced? Quite a bit, actually. For such parents, Wallerstein offers the following advice. First, stay strong. The child should be assured that she is not suddenly responsible for her parents' emotional well-being. Two, provide continuity for the child, maintaining her usual schedule of activities. Try to keep her in the same playgroup, the same milieu, among familiar faces and accustomed scenes. Lastly, don't let your own search for new love preoccupy you at the child's expense.

Her chief message to married parents is clear: suck it up if you possibly can, and stick it out. But even if you agree with Wallerstein, how realistic is such spartan advice? The experts disagree. Then again, her advice is not for experts. It's directed at people bickering in their kitchen and staring up at the ceiling of their bedroom. It's directed at parents who have already divorced and are sitting alone in front of the TV, contemplating a second try.

The truth and usefulness of Wallerstein's findings will be tested in houses and apartments, in parks and playgrounds, not in sterile think tanks. Someday, assuming we're in a mood to listen, millions of children will give us the results.

Breaking Up Is Hard to Do[3]

By Mubarak Dahir
The Advocate, September 11, 2001

During her nearly 20-year relationship, Jennifer Levinson considered herself married in every sense to her partner, Kathy Levinson.

On many counts, the Levinsons mimicked the Ozzie and Harriet model of the American family: While Kathy moved up the corporate ladder to become chief operating officer of E*TRADE, the wildly successful online brokerage firm, Jennifer stayed at home and took care of their two children and the house. "If you go back to the 1950s model, Kathy was the husband, and I was the wife," Jennifer says.

There was, of course, at least one crucial difference between Kathy and Jennifer and Ozzie and Harriet: Kathy and Jennifer didn't have a marriage license.

There are many indications, however, that they would have married if it were legal. Though Kathy is the biological mother of their two young children, Jennifer adopted them. Jennifer even legally changed her last name to match Kathy's.

And last year their personal relationship turned highly public when Californians were asked to vote for a ban on gay and lesbian marriage. The Levinsons became national poster girls for same-sex marriage, speaking out against the referendum and forking over $300,000—as well as helping to raise hundreds of thousands more—to help finance the unsuccessful campaign to defeat it.

Until the two broke up in April 2000, Jennifer says she thought the relationship "was equal in every way—including financially." But ever since the bitter split, the two have been locked in an acrimonious who-gets-what squabble. When Kathy retired in May 2000 from E*TRADE, her net worth was estimated at as much as $40 million. And as Kathy's de facto wife, Jennifer says she deserves half of everything.

But *married* is a legal term, and "we [gays and lesbians] still don't have it," says Cliff Staton, a spokesman for Kathy Levinson. (Levinson declined to talk with *The Advocate*.) "We're not guaranteed the rights of married people," he says—including the same rules of divorce.

With the exception of Vermont, where a same-sex couple wanting to dissolve its civil union can go through the same family court system as married couples wanting a divorce, there is precious little legal framework for same-sex couples who call it quits.

"At best," says Suzanne Goldberg, an assistant professor of law at Rutgers University in New Jersey and a family law expert, "the law treats a same-sex breakup as a business deal between two people about property. It's highly dependent on whatever separation agreement the couple may have. It's done without the complex background rules of divorce, which take into account the context of sacrifices and decisions two people make as a family unit. Divorce rules have evolved to ensure the partner in the weaker financial position is not left penniless. But when gay and lesbian couples separate, it boils down to who holds the purse strings."

> *"When gay and lesbian couples separate, it boils down to who holds the purse strings."—* Suzanne Goldberg, Rutgers University.

The irony, of course, is that "one of the best arguments for gay people's freedom to marry is divorce," says Evan Wolfson, director of the Freedom to Marry Project in New York City.

"When straight people marry, it's understood that they acquire certain property rights simply as part of the status of marriage," says Erica Bell, an out lesbian partner at the New York law firm Weiss, Buell, and Bell. "As long as gays and lesbians are denied the right to marry, we're denied those property rights as well. It's all about status—plainly put, we just don't have it." Just like in marriage law, she says, gay people are virtually invisible in divorce, legally speaking.

In only one state besides Vermont has there been significant legal recognition for gays and lesbians who end their relationships. Leaning on a series of laws known as "equitable" or "fairness" doctrine, a Washington State appellate court ruled in the late 1990s that unmarried partners are presumed entitled to half of the couple's combined assets, even without a written or oral contract.

Based on that ruling, some Washington municipalities are applying family law principles to lesbian and gay couples, says Frederick Hertz, an Oakland, Calif., lawyer and one of the nation's leading experts on gay and lesbian divorce. However, he cautions, the Washington ruling involved an unmarried heterosexual couple, "so there is still fierce debate if it applies to gays or not."

Hertz is the author of *Legal Affairs: Essential Advice for Same-Sex Couples* and also is representing Jennifer Levinson in her lawsuit against Kathy Levinson. He says there are about five states in which gay people have absolutely no legal recourse when seeking redress during a separation. In at least three other states (Minnesota, Texas, and New York), any court claim must be based on the violation of a written agreement.

In most states unmarried couples—straight or gay—can theoretically make claims on money or property, based on agreements that are written or verbal or can be proved by patterns of conduct. These claims are duked out in civil court rather than family court, and they must be based on the individual state's contract laws. "And that means that, every step of the way, the legal system favors the one with the power, the one with the assets," Hertz says.

Jerry Chasen, a principal with Miami law firm Chasen and Associates, agrees. "It's almost always the person without the money who seeks legal help" in a gay or lesbian breakup, and that person "is trying to assert his or her rights as if they were in a legally recognized union," he says. Unfortunately, he adds, "they often don't have a legal leg to stand on. The law just doesn't provide any kind of recognition for this kind of relationship—and thus no recognition when the relationships fall apart. An intimate [same-sex] relationship doesn't mean squat to the law."

Though the rules vary widely from state to state, Hertz says that, in general, "divorce law is the most enlightened law in America." Women, typically at an economic disadvantage in heterosexual marriages, are no longer at the mercy of their husbands, he says. But when gays and lesbians sever their relationships, "the weakest one gets screwed. The absence of marriage leaves us vulnerable."

> *"The legal system favors the one with the power, the one with the assets."*— **Frederick Hertz, lawyer.**

Vulnerable is exactly how "Ben" (who asked that his real name not be used) says he felt when he found himself in the midst of an acrid breakup with his partner of 10 years. The couple's $350,000 home in a wealthy Philadelphia suburb was in both their names, and the pair had a verbal agreement that they would divide the sale of the house down the middle should they ever go their separate ways. But Ben says that during the breakup, his partner said several times that he thought he deserved the lion's share from the house's sale.

When Ben and his partner first moved in together, both men earned roughly equal incomes. Within their first year as a couple they purchased their first house. Ben footed the entire $80,000 down payment, and the two split the mortgage payments 50–50.

A year and a half later, Ben's partner inherited $750,000 and a paid-off family home. Using the proceeds from the sale of the family home plus the profit from the sale of the house they lived in, the couple upgraded to a larger place. Again, they split the mortgage payments equally. Ben's partner did pay a higher percentage of the utilities and upkeep, but Ben says he himself was the handyman who kept the place in shape.

Ben was troubled when he says his ex began making noises about getting more than half the value of their shared property. "We never had a written agreement. I was worried he was going to show up at the settlement table and demand 75% of the profits, and I knew a judge wasn't going to look at two men the same way he would a married couple."

To protect himself, Ben hired a lawyer who basically threatened to out Ben's partner at work if he tried to claim more than his fair share. "It was essentially blackmail," Ben says. "But I couldn't depend on the laws, and this was fair. If I didn't do something to protect myself, I might have been ripped off."

Today, Ben and his current partner share a home in Delaware. Because Ben's partner has a spotty credit history, the couple decided to put the house solely in Ben's name. However, Ben insisted they draw up legal documents spelling out that they each own a 50% share. "I wanted my partner to feel a sense of ownership even though his name isn't on the mortgage," Ben says. "And I didn't ever want him to feel the way I had."

But Ben and his partner are the exception rather than the rule, most legal experts agree. "It's easy to understand why so few gay and lesbian couples avoid the topic," Goldberg says. "No one wants to think about the possibility of breaking up when they are in love." Furthermore, as Chasen points out, even if a couple manages to broach the subject, there's no guarantee that the person in the weaker financial position will get a fair deal.

The Levinson case demonstrates that drawing up legal documents doesn't guarantee that confrontation will be avoided. Jennifer Levinson says that in 1989 she and Kathy drew up a partnership agreement outlining their finances: "But it was prepared when we were both working and there wasn't much disparity between our incomes, before we had children, before I quit my job to take care of our home affairs, and before we had wealth." Since that time, she adds, "our lives changed dramatically: I quit work, raised the kids, and kept house, while she got a gazillion stock options." Although she did not give specifics about the agreement, she says it "is outdated" and would leave her practically penniless.

Staton, Kathy Levinson's spokesman, disputes Jennifer's version. "Kathy's view is that because they were unable to get married, they created a series of contracts to guide and define their relationship," he says. Staton describes the couple's written financial agreement as being "worth millions of dollars to Jennifer" but says that she is now trying to alter the terms of the agreement in hopes of winning more money.

Under California law, married couples split the family assets 50–50 when divorcing, in the absence of an agreement to the contrary. Jennifer Levinson says she should not deserve less simply because her relationship was to a woman rather than a man. (The couple share custody of their 5- and 8-year-old children.)

"If we were married and she was the man, there's no question this would absolutely be easier," Jennifer says. "But because the courts didn't recognize me and Kathy and the kids as a family, it's applying business and contract law to my marriage. That's devastating and demeaning."

With evident sadness she adds, "Mine is the perfect example of why we need all the rights of marriage—including divorce."

IV. Families in Crisis

Editor's Introduction

T he four articles in this section discuss various problems facing the modern American family. The struggle to balance work, family, and outside commitments has intensified in recent years, with even the youngest children pulled between myriad activities. With the massive changes to American society since World War II and the increased independence and spending power of children and teenagers, many parents find it difficult to set firm boundaries for their offspring. Other concerns range from worrying about the family's finances, to more dire fears about the sexual, physical, and/or emotional abuse of family members, including children, spouses, and domestic partners.

In "More Americans Put Families Ahead of Work" by Stephanie Armour, the balance between work and family is addressed. Making time for family is a growing priority for many workers disillusioned by layoffs, corporate scandal, and waning company loyalty. Many Generation X-ers have little hesitation about leaving one company for another if their employers are not flexible about giving them time with their families. Meanwhile, Baby Boomers often need more time away from work to care both for children and aging parents. The September 11, 2001, terrorist attacks were also a wake-up call for many people who put in long hours at the office to the detriment of their family lives.

Jane Yager describes the difficulties of those in low-income jobs to raise a family and find good, affordable child care in her article "Mission Impossible." While many champions of welfare reform claim that personal responsibility is the hallmark of the new system, Yager contends that they have little feeling for the needs of poor children, who will suffer through no fault of their own if a parent is unable to find or keep a job.

"Stifled Screams" by Armstrong Williams provides a frightening picture of domestic violence and details the problems facing abuse victims who seek help. The difficulty in gaining a restraining order, unresponsive police, and the lack of adequate women's shelters are just a few of the difficulties victims face. More funding, a better police response, and training doctors to provide help to abuse victims are suggested remedies.

"Who's in Charge Here?" recounts the struggles of many parents to set limits for their children. The author searches for factors that may be contributing to an increase in "spoiled" children, including parental behavior and the media. The attitudes of Baby Boomer parents, known for challenging accepted modes of conduct when they were younger and who therefore may have a hard time being strict with their own children, are one aspect of the problem. In addition, children are now the focus of intense marketing campaigns, absorbing consumer messages at school, sporting events, and while watching their favorite programs after school, from *SpongeBob SquarePants* to *Total Request Live*. The author compares overindulged youths with those who show signs of being well-adjusted members of society, and she describes a growing movement among parents determined not to spoil their children and who are setting stricter boundaries for them.

More Americans Put Families Ahead of Work[1]

By Stephanie Armour
USA Today, December 5, 2002

Family is important to Patrick Snow.

It's so important that he'll stop working in the afternoon to coach his sons' basketball games. It's so important he's brought up family in job interviews, candidly telling managers he needs to limit work hours so he can be with his two boys.

He knows it means his job in high-tech sales could suffer, but that doesn't matter to him. Family is so important, he says, he'd leave any employer who didn't understand.

"If my company doesn't like it, I'll find another job," says Snow, 33, of Bainbridge Island, Wash. He is also a speaker, coach and author of *Creating Your Own Destiny*.

"Employees used to be willing to sacrifice because of things like stock options. Now, they're fed up. They realize that family is the only stabilizing force in this turbulent economy," he says.

Employees have long struggled to balance work and family, but the economic slowdown is now tilting the scales in favor of home. Making time for family isn't just important for a few employees like Snow—it's a growing priority for many workers disillusioned by layoffs, corporate scandal and waning company loyalty.

It's also a challenge bedeviling employers. Companies facing profit pressures need to squeeze more work out of fewer employees, but they risk retention problems if they appear insensitive to their staffs' family needs.

That's because 70% of workers don't think there is a healthy balance between work and personal life, according to a poll of 1,626 respondents by online job board TrueCareers, based in Reston, Va. And more than half are considering looking for a new job because of problems coping with both.

"There's a real shift," says Debra Major, an associate professor of psychology at Old Dominion University in Norfolk, Va. "In this economy, working 70 hours a week no longer makes a difference in how much you get compensated or how fast you advance. Employees want to prioritize their own values, not the values that the company says are important."

Consider other national studies:

---

1. Copyright © 2002, *USA Today*. Reprinted with permission.

- Finding time for family is a more pressing concern than layoffs. More than 30% of employees said balancing work and family demands was a top concern in a May survey of 567 full-time employees by staffing services firm OfficeTeam, based in Menlo Park, Calif. That eclipses the 22% who said job security was a top concern.

- Almost three times as many employees say family is their top priority as those who list work as a top priority, according to a survey of more than 1,000 employees by Atlanta-based staffing firm Randstad North America and market research firm RoperASW.

- Nearly twice as many employees took sick days for personal needs in 2002 as did so last year, according to a survey by human-resource and employment-law information provider CCH of 333 human resource professionals in 43 states and the District of Columbia.

Tugged in Every Direction

It's not that work is no longer important. Job insecurity wrought by the down economy means some workers are clocking longer hours and sacrificing even more in a bid to avoid layoffs. Many feel less able to refuse bosses' requests that they relocate, travel or give up vacation to get work done.

"People are like a puppet being pulled in every direction," says Stephen Covey, author of motivational books such as *The 7 Habits of Highly Effective People*. "People have re-prioritized in their minds and hearts, but the economic struggles and all the uncertainty have people torn between what they'd like to do and what they have to do."

Several factors are pushing family to the forefront and prompting many workers to prioritize home, even if that decision means paying a professional price.

Psychologists, researchers and other workplace experts credit the shift to the changing priorities of a younger generation, family burdens facing baby boomers, the aftereffects of the Sept. 11 attacks and a backlash against the profit-making fixation of the late 1990s.

Part of the shift is simply generational change. As Generation X and Y employees start families, they are increasingly likely to place importance on the home front, research shows.

More than 85% of Gen X women say having a loving family is extremely important, compared with 18% who put the priority on earning a great deal of money, according to a study by research group Catalyst, which is based in New York.

Also driving the emphasis on family are baby boomers, who are increasingly likely to be part of the so-called "sandwich generation" caring for both children and older relatives.

More than 25% of adults have provided care for a chronically ill, disabled or aged family member or friend during the past year, according to the National Family Caregivers Association. Based on current Census data, that translates into more than 50 million people.

For those employees, there's no choice but to put family first. And it's an issue employers are paying attention to—more than 20% of companies offer elder-care referral services, according to the Society for Human Resource Management. That's up from 15% in 1998.

> ### *Nearly 80% of Americans say their family is more of a priority since Sept. 11.*

Nipping Hours at Work

Mary Murphy-Hoye, 45, curtailed her work hours and changed job duties within Intel. That has allowed her more time to spend with her father, who is temporarily living with her family in Phoenix.

But the new focus she's put on family isn't just a result of elder-care needs. As it was for many Americans, the re-prioritization was shaped by the events of Sept. 11. Workers' resolve to put family first hasn't faded with the passage of time.

In a report this year by New York-based American Demographics and Greenwich, Conn.-based marketing research firm NFO World-Group, nearly 80% of Americans say their family is more of a priority since Sept. 11, compared with 70% who said the same in October 2001. The poll of 2,500 adults found respondents with children were even more stalwart in their determination to prioritize family.

For Murphy-Hoye, a mother of two boys (Patrick, 8, and Thomas, 11), there have been big changes. The engineer used to work on site in Sacramento, and she traveled. But in June of 2001, she switched jobs to focus on research and work from home. She also trimmed her schedule and puts in fewer hours each day.

"We got a wake-up call," says Murphy-Hoye about Sept. 11. "Everything is about simplifying and getting back to what's really important. I don't feel quite as exhausted as I did before. I'm a lot more in touch with my kids."

Employers Adjust

The emphasis on family isn't lost on employers. Despite the recession, nearly all forms of work-life programs saw modest growth in the past year, according to a May survey of 945 major U.S. employers by Hewitt Associates, an outsourcing and consulting firm based in Lincolnshire, Ill.

These benefits, such as flexible work schedules and job sharing, often cost little but provide a big return.

At New York Life Insurance, work-life benefits include on-site back-up child care, adoption assistance, flexible schedules and an employee health department.

"We've been committed to work-life for many years now," says Angela Coleman, vice president of human resources at New York Life. "We want programs that meet the needs of our employees. It's about attracting and recruiting, but also about retaining employees."

At biotechnology company Genentech, programs include a subsidized child care center near the headquarters in South San Francisco, an on-site hair salon, domestic partner benefits and sabbatical programs that provide six weeks off at full pay after every six consecutive years of service.

"They're very important," says Stephanie Ashe, a spokeswoman at Genentech. "We ask a lot of our employees, but in return, we have many, many programs to help employees with work-life balance."

Kathy Eckert knows first-hand just how flexible some companies will be. After staying home with children Sarah, 10, and Jason, 7, she took a public relations job at software development company Benefitfocus. She was willing to accept the job in large part because the company catered to her family needs. Her bosses let her work 15 to 20 hours a week and give her leave as needed to attend her children's school events. Meetings are set around her schedule.

Just before Thanksgiving, her daughter's fourth-grade class staged a parade. On her way to work, Eckert took 45 minutes to drop in at the school and watch.

"No one was watching a clock," says Eckert, 42. "My family knows I work. My husband is appreciative of the extra income, yet my husband and children know they come first."

Employee Benefits Grow

Percentage of employers offering family-friendly benefits:

	1998	2002
Dependent care flexible spending account	60%	70%
Flextime	56%	64%
Telecommuting	25%	33%
Compressed workweek	23%	33%
Bring child to work in emergency	19%	30%
Elder-care referral service	15%	21%
Adoption assistance	12%	21%
Lactation program/designated area	5%	19%

Shawn Jenkins, president and CEO of Benefitfocus in Mount Pleasant, S.C., says designing a position to be so flexible was a new endeavor for his company. "The result is an employee who is very focused when she is here, because when she wants to put family first, she can."

Lowered Expectations

Though the emphasis on family is shaped by demographics and events such as Sept. 11, the economy is also a major driver, experts say.

Expectations have changed. During the boom years of the dot-com era, pay raises were on the way up. More than 70% of college students polled said they expected to someday be millionaires, according to a 2000 Ernst & Young survey. There was money to be made in long hours on the job.

Now, advancement is blocked because fewer employees are changing jobs. Raises are paltry. And workers realize there's no guarantee their extra effort on the job will guarantee job security. Sacrifices don't seem as worth it.

Suddenly, family seems top priority.

It's what's most important to Luis Valdes, a vice president and consulting psychologist with management consulting firm Turknett Leadership Group, based in Atlanta.

He had been on the road three to four days a week, but after a spell at home with a mild illness, he realized he wanted more time to be with his three children, Timothy, 14, Jordan, 4, and Liana, 9 months. Now, he's focused on building a local consulting practice instead of being on the road.

"I wanted to be involved with my kids, and I was missing big parts of their lives," says Valdes, 47. "Now, my relationship with them is much better."

It's what's most important to Viveca Woods, 31, of New York, who six months ago left a secure job at a public relations agency to start a consultancy, VMW Public Relations. She can work from home and have a flexible schedule with daughter, Brittany, 4, and 1-year-old son, Logan.

"I love to work, but I want to be a very good mom," she says. "It was a risk, but my family is important."

Mission Impossible[2]

BY JANE YAGER
DOLLARS & SENSE, SEPTEMBER/OCTOBER 2002

One morning, a Denver employer received a call from an employee. The employee, a mother of a young child, could not come to work that day because she had run out of diapers for her baby. Her child care center required parents to bring their own diapers, but the mother had no money to buy them. Her only option was to stay home, losing at best a day's income and at worst her job. Hearing this story, the supervisor rushed out to buy a pack of diapers and deliver it to the daycare center. The employer later admitted that she would have punished or even fired the worker were it not for the personal bond between the two: "Unless I had that kind of relationship with her, so that she would trust me to tell what is going on, I would have just been angry and assumed she is screwing up."

For the post-welfare-reform low-income families featured in the 2002 report "Raising Families and Keeping Jobs in Low-Income America: It Just Doesn't Work," the Denver mother's story offers a best-case scenario. It's a given that the mother will not earn enough money to meet the child's needs, that missing work for a sick child might get her fired, and that child care arrangements will be unstable. The only real variable is the boss's degree of sympathy and flexibility.

The Across the Boundaries Project, a joint program of the 9 to 5 Association and the Radcliffe Public Policy Center, has undertaken a two-year study of the work–family conflicts that low-income working parents face in the wake of welfare reform. In 2000 and 2001, the project conducted interviews with hundreds of low-income parents, their employers, and their child care providers in three cities: Milwaukee, Denver, and Boston.

The report shows that "It Just Doesn't Work" on two counts: child care arrangements and jobs are both failing low-income families. Parents, child care workers, and employers all describe child care arrangements as makeshift and inherently unstable, "not a routine but a complex orchestra." Parents patch together partial days at expensive daycare centers with informal care by relatives and older children. In many cases, no two days have the same routine, and informal arrangements break down, requiring parents to leave work. Employers complain about workers making phone calls during their breaks to check that their children made it safely to

2. Reprinted by permission of *Dollars & Sense*, a progressive economics magazine <www.dollarsandsense.org>.

after-school care. One employer said that when she "thinks of it in terms of being a mother," she knows she should not punish parents who leave work to care for children, but then admitted that she has fired mothers for staying home with sick children. Another employer, after allowing that he could never manage the balancing act that low-income parents attempt, complained, "these people don't seem to know how to be organized." Many of the employers surveyed said that they had punished or fired a worker for leaving work to deal with a child care situation.

With Americans now working longer hours than workers in any other industrialized country, the work–family time crunch is a familiar story. When it comes to college educated middle-class women, the public debate has focused on concerns about "mommy-tracking," or lowered career expectations for mothers in dual-earner households. Some private employers have relieved work–family conflict with programs like job-sharing, telecommuting, and flextime, but these options are rarely available in the service-sector, small-employer, and entry-level jobs that employ low-wage workers. Even when such programs are available, low-income workers are unlikely to use them: who can telecommute without owning a personal computer?

With Americans now working longer hours than workers in any other industrialized country, the work–family time crunch is a familiar story.

Low-income Americans' work and family lives are left out of this relatively sympathetic debate. Poor women with children are discussed instead in punitive, paternalistic terms of single motherhood and personal irresponsibility. Robert Rector of the Heritage Foundation, a chief architect of welfare reform, recently wrote, "Members of Congress must recognize three rules for escaping poverty in America; no one who follows them will be 'chronically poor': a) finish high school; b) get a job—any job—and stick with it; and c) do not have children outside of marriage." Get-tough recommendations like this so dominate the mainstream policy debate on welfare that the binds faced by low-income workers with children receive little attention. "Raising Families and Keeping Jobs . . ." is the only major report since 1996 to address work–family conflicts in low-income families.

For many low-income workers, frequent job turnover compounds the anxiety of unstable child care. Parents, child care workers, and employers all mentioned job turnover as a major problem. Most of the parents in the study worked in personal service, clerical, retail, or light manufacturing jobs. As a rule, they earned less than $10 an hour and had no vacation or sick time, no health insurance, and no union representation. Workers and employers agreed that there was not much motivation to remain at a job for long: those who stuck around had little chance of gaining promotions, benefits or higher wages. One employer, asked about her employees' chances of advancement, said, "I suppose the only way to do better is to leave [my place of employment] and try to get something better. . . . Really, even if you're a good worker

"These women shouldn't have a child if they can't afford to."—Boston employer.

and all. . . . without more school they aren't going anywhere." A Milwaukee mother agreed: "There is no light at the end of this tunnel . . . it just goes on and on."

Many parents found that switching jobs was the only way to adjust their work schedules to meet child care needs. The pursuit of a "generous" boss, most often defined as one who would let workers bring their children to work, was another common motivation for switching jobs. In a sea of low-paying, dead-end jobs, a boss's attitude toward child care determined a job's desirability. A Milwaukee mother said that she stayed at her $7.50 per hour job because it gives her "some flexibility to be with my children. That's the only reason I'm still there."

Much to the surprise of researchers, single mothers interviewed mentioned prejudice against single mothers in the workplace as often as they mentioned racism in the workplace. (Seventy percent of the single mothers who participated in the study were women of color.) The moralistic climate of welfare reform has seeped into the women's daily lives. Many mothers reported that child care workers and employers treated them unsympathetically because they were single mothers. Employers' comments confirmed this impression. "These women shouldn't have a child if they can't afford to," a Boston employer said.

But the study's most surprising finding was the degree of agreement among parents, employers, and child care providers. All agreed that the way things are now just doesn't work; that unstable child care strategies hurt employment; that low-income parents don't have enough time for their children; and that workers need greater flexibility. Employers and workers only disagreed about one thing: whether employers are responsible to their employees for anything more than the bottom line. "We are not running a social program here," one Boston temp agency supervisor said repeatedly. All the more reason that low-income workers need the policy changes that the report recommends: the right to collective bargaining, a higher wage floor, expansion of Family Medical Leave Act benefits, access to affordable high-quality child care, and greater job flexibility and benefits for part-time workers. Reconciling jobs with the needs of families will take something a lot more substantial than bosses who pitch in for the diapers their employees can't afford.

Stifled Screams[3]

By Armstrong Williams
New York Amsterdam News, March 7, 2002

Stephanie Rodriguez knew why her husband beat her. He was impassioned and jealous. And God wanted her beat up—that much was clear.

So she curled into his love and anger, just as her own mother had done before finally committing suicide.

Then one day, Rodriguez's husband began whipping their 10-year-old daughter with his belt because she could not find her notebook. The father calmly explained that he would continue to beat her every five minutes until she found the notebook. This was for her own good, he reasoned.

Her eyes full of tears, the child rummaged through the house. Every five minutes, the father yanked her up and began yet another beating. Her arms and back swelled with welts. Rodriguez joined in the frantic search but the notebook was lost.

They huddled together and prayed. It did not matter. Every five minutes, the father came stalking down the hall.

Finally, Rodriguez snatched a wooden plank from the kitchen and cracked it over her husband's head. He stumbled backwards. The plank dropped. He regained his composure, then began to beat his wife and child relentlessly.

Eventually, the paramedics had to wheel their crumpled bodies from the house.

The scene is chillingly common.

Every 15 seconds in the United States, a woman is physically assaulted by her husband, boyfriend or live-in partner.

For those who fall victim to this brutal and arbitrary violence, the state offers a host of legal protections, starting with having the courts issue a restraining order.

Just one thing: Since judges issue restraining orders, the complaint must be lodged during regular business hours. Should you have the misfortune of getting assaulted during off-hours, you will likely be unable to secure this sort of legal protection, leaving the risk of domestic violence unacceptably high.

"I don't know anyone who has gotten a restraining order on an evening or weekend," sighed Nancy Meyer, executive director of the D.C. Coalition Against Domestic Violence. "If it's not during

---

business hours, you are out of luck. And in places like D.C., the police response is abysmal. So it's not only a matter of not getting a restraining order, but you can't even get a response."

> *Doctors need to be more usefully engaged in the battle against domestic abuse.*

Caitlin Finnegan, co-director of community education with My Sister's Place, says that the D.C. Superior Court sees more than 30 women a day looking for emergency assistance and protective orders. Sadly, D.C. maintains only two shelters, which offer less than 50 beds. Such limited space fills quickly. In which case, Finnegan has been known to shuttle victims around town—to homeless shelters and other facilities that can provide temporary lodging. She admits, however, that makeshift responses don't provide the targeted assistance and intervention that's necessary to break the cycle of violence.

What's really needed is a straightforward increase in funding. Sadly, efforts to corral additional money are hamstrung by the perception that domestic abuse is no longer a serious problem. "I think what really has happened," observed Meyer, "is that domestic violence has become part of a web of social ills, so the issue has become invisible in a broad public-policy sense."

That does not bode well for the 2.5 million women that the Justice Department estimates are abused annually. Nor does it bode well for adolescent victims of physical and sexual assault, who are six to nine times more likely to commit suicide.

While we wait for additional funds, there are still some very practical things we can do to affect change, beginning with greater accountability for police response times and a recommitment to action within our own communities. We may not be able to end domestic violence, but we can organize on the grassroots level and work to secure comprehensive involvement from community-based organizations, rather than expecting the state to have all of the answers.

Finnegan also observed that doctors need to be more usefully engaged in the battle against domestic abuse. "I have doctors tell me all the time, 'Look, I have patients I know are being abused; I just don't know what to say to them.'"

Finnegan attributes this silence to cultural norms that dissuade medical professionals from prying into their patients' personal matters.

Plainly, doctors need to be trained to be more proactive in suggesting preventive methods.

The alternative is to leave the victims of domestic abuse to their own devices, and to invite yet more disaster into our homes.

Who's in Charge Here?[4]

By Nancy Gibbs
TIME, August 6, 2001

Here is a parenting parable for our age. Carla Wagner, 17, of Coral Gables, Fla., spent the afternoon drinking the tequila she charged on her American Express Gold Card before speeding off in her high-performance Audi A4. She was dialing her cell phone when she ran over Helen Marie Witty, a 16-year-old honor student who was out Rollerblading. Charged with drunken driving and manslaughter, Carla was given a trial date—at which point her parents asked the judge whether it would be O.K. if Carla went ahead and spent the summer in Paris, as she usually does.

That settled it, as far as Mark Marion and Diane Sanchez, also of Coral Gables, were concerned. Their daughter Ariana, then 17, knew Carla, who was described in the local papers as the "poster child for spoiled teens." Ariana too had wanted a sports car for her 16th birthday, not an unreasonable expectation for a girl with a $2,000 Cartier watch whose bedroom had just had a $10,000 make-over. But Ariana's parents had already reached that moment that parents reach, when they wage a little war on themselves and their values and their neighbors and emerge with a new resolve.

Maybe Ariana would just have to wait for a car, they decided, wait until she had finished school and earned good grades and done volunteer work at the hospital. "We needed to get off the roller coaster," says Diane, and even her daughter agrees. "For my parents' generation, to even have a car when you were a teenager was a big deal," Ariana says. "Today, if it's not a Mercedes, it's not special." She pauses. "I think," she observes, "we lost the antimate-rialistic philosophy they had. . . . But then, it seems, so did they."

Even their children level the charge at the baby boomers: that members of history's most indulged generation are setting new records when it comes to indulging their kids. The indictment gathered force during the roaring '90s. A TIME/CNN poll finds that 80% of people think kids today are more spoiled than kids of 10 or 15 years ago, and two-thirds of parents admit that their kids are spoiled. In New York City it's the Bar Mitzvah where 'N Sync was the band; in Houston it's a catered $20,000 pink-themed party for 50 seven-year-old girls who all wore mink coats, like their moms. In Morton Grove, Ill., it's grade school teachers handing out candy and yo-yos on Fridays to kids who actually managed to obey the rules that week. Go to the mall or a concert or a restaurant and you can find them in the wild, the kids who have never been told no, whose sense of power and entitlement leaves onlookers breathless, the sand-kicking, foot-stomping, arm-twisting, wheedling, whining despots whose parents presumably deserve the company of the monsters they, after all, created.

It is so tempting to accept the cartoon version of modern boomer parenting that it is easy to miss the passionate debate underneath it. Leave aside the extremes, the lazy parents who set no bounds and the gifted ones who are naturally wise when it comes to kids. In between you hear the conversation, the unending concern and confusion over where and how to draw the lines. Have we gone too far, given kids more power than they can handle and more stuff than they can possibly need? Should we negotiate with our children or just inform them of the rules? Is $20 too much for lunch money? What chores should kids have to do, and which are extra credit? Can you treat them with respect without sacrificing your authority? Cheer them on without driving them too hard? Set them free—but still set limits?

Some of these are eternal questions. Today's parents may often get the answers wrong, but it's also wrong to say they're not even try-

---

> ### *It is so tempting to accept the cartoon version of modern boomer parenting that it is easy to miss the passionate debate underneath it.*

---

ing. You don't have to get far into a conversation with parents to hear them wrestling with these issues. And you don't have to look hard to see a rebellion brewing. Just as the wobbling economy of the past year made conspicuous consumption a little less conspicuous, it also gave parents an excuse to do what they have wanted to do anyway: say no to the $140 sneakers, fire the gardener, have junior mow the lawn. The *Wall Street Journal* calls it the Kid Recession: overall consumer spending rose slightly last year, but it dropped about a third among 8- to 24-year-olds. The *Journal* cited a November survey that found that 12% of kids said their allowance had been cut in recent months, while 16% received fewer gifts.

This is a war waged block by block, house by house. If it is too much to try to battle the forces of Hollywood or Madison Avenue or the Nintendo Corp., at least you can resolve that just because the kids down the street watch unlimited TV doesn't mean your kids should too. You can enforce a curfew, assign some chores and try hard to have dinner together regularly. And then hope that the experts are right when they say that what kids mainly need is time and attention and love, none of which takes American Express.

The historians and psychologists have lots of theories about how we got here, but some perennial truths persist: every generation thinks the next one is too slack; every parent reinvents the job. Parenthood, like childhood, is a journey of discovery. You set off from your memories of being a kid, all the blessings, all the scars. You overreact, improvise and over time maybe learn what works; with luck you improve. It is characteristic of the baby boomers to imagine themselves the first to take this trip, to pack so many guidebooks to read along the way and to try to minimize any discomfort.

But a lot about being a millennial parent is actually new, and hard. Prosperity is a great gift, and these are lucky, peaceful times, but in some respects it is more difficult to be a parent now than when our parents were at the wheel. Today's prosperity has been fueled by people working longer hours than ever, and it is especially challenging to parent creatively and well when you're strung out and exhausted. The extended-family structure that once shared the burdens and reinforced values has frayed. Nothing breeds wretched excess like divorced parents competing with each other and feeling guilty to boot. It's not an option, as it once was, to let kids roam free outside after school, bike over to a friend's house, hang out with cousins or grandparents. The streets are not safe and the family is scattered, so kids are often left alone, inside, with the TV and all its messages.

Advertising targets children as never before, creating cravings that are hard to ignore but impossible to satisfy. These days $3 billion is spent annually on advertising that is directed at kids—more than 20 times the amount a decade ago. Nearly half of all U.S. parents say their kids ask for things by brand names by age 5. "I might mention to a child that the dress she is wearing is cute," says Marci Sperling Flynn, a preschool director in Oak Park, Ill., "and she'll say, 'It's Calvin Klein.' Kids shouldn't know about designers at age 4. They should be oblivious to this stuff."

Children have never wielded this much power in the marketplace. In 1984 children were estimated to influence about $50 billion of U.S. parents' purchases; the figure is expected to approach $300 billion this year. According to the Maryland-based Center for a New American Dream, which dispenses antidotes for raging consumerism, two-thirds of parents say their kids define their self-worth in terms of possessions; half say their kids prefer to go to a shopping mall than to go hiking or on a family outing; and a majority admit to buying their children products they disapprove of—products that may even be bad for them—because the kids said they "needed" the items to fit in with their friends.

Peer pressure can hit lower-income families especially hard. George Valadez, a hot-dog and beer vendor at Chicago's Wrigley Field, has sole custody of his three young kids. His concept of being a good provider is to pour every spare cent into them. The family's two-bedroom apartment is crammed with five television sets, three video-game consoles and two VCRs. Next month his kids want to attend a church camp in Michigan that costs $100 a child. So two weeks ago, abandoning their custom of giving away outgrown clothes and toys to neighbors, the family held its first yard sale to raise cash.

Technology also contributes to the erosion of parental authority. Video games are about letting kids manipulate reality, bend it to their will, which means that when they get up at last from the console, the loss of power is hard to handle. You can't click your little brother out of existence. Plus, no generation has had access to this much information, along with the ability to share it and twist it. Teenagers can re-create themselves, invent a new identity online, escape the boundaries of the household into a very private online world with few guardrails. As Michael Lewis argues in his new book, *Next: The Future Just Happened*, a world in which 14-year-olds can manipulate the stock market and 19-year-olds can threaten the whole music industry represents a huge shift in the balance of power.

In some ways the baby boomers were uniquely ill equipped to handle such broad parenting challenges. So eager to Question Authority when they were flower children, the boomers are reluctant to exer-

---

"What parents need to understand is that their primary job is being a parent, not being their kids' friend."—Wade Horn, clinical child psychologist.

---

cise it now. "This is overly harsh, overly cynical, but there's a reason why the baby-boom generation has been called the Me generation," says Wade Horn, a clinical child psychologist and President Bush's assistant secretary for family support at the Department of Health and Human Services. "They spent the 1950s being spoiled, spent the 1960s having a decade-long temper tantrum because the world was not precisely as they wanted it to be, spent the 1970s having the best sex and drugs they could find, the 1980s acquiring things and the 1990s trying to have the most perfect children. And not because they felt an obligation to the next generation to rear them to be healthy, well-adjusted adults, but because they wanted to have bragging rights."

That's the baby-boomer indictment in a nutshell, but there's a more benign way to interpret this generation's parenting. Those who grew up with emotionally remote parents who rarely got right down on the floor to play, who wouldn't think of listening respectfully to their six-year-old's opinions or explain why the rules are what they are, have tried to build a very different bond with their children. They are far more fluent in the language of emotional trauma and intent on not repeating their parents' mistakes. What's more, having prolonged childhoods, many parents today identify powerfully with their kids. But as Horn notes, "It's difficult to set limits with your children if your primary goal is to be liked. What parents need to understand is that their primary job is being a parent, not being their kids' friend."

It is a natural, primitive instinct to want to make your child happy and protect him from harm or pain. But that instinct, if not tempered, also comes with a cost. Adolescents can't learn to become emotionally resilient if they don't get any practice with frustration or failure inside their protective cocoons. Sean Stevenson, a fifth-grade teacher in Montgomery County, Md., says parents always say they want discipline and order in the classroom, but if it's their child who breaks the rules, they want an exemption. "They don't want the punishment to be enforced," says Stevenson. "They want to excuse the behavior. 'It's something in the child's past. Something else set him off. He just needs to be told, and it won't happen again.'"

In September, Harvard psychologist Dan Kindlon, co-author of the best-selling 1999 book *Raising Cain*, will publish *Too Much of a Good Thing: Raising Children of Character in an Indulgent Age*, in which he warns parents against spoiling their children either materially or emotionally, against trying to make kids' lives perfect. Using the body's immune system as a metaphor, Kindlon argues, "The body cannot learn to adapt to stress unless it experiences it. Indulged children are often less able to cope with stress because their parents have created an atmosphere where their whims are indulged, where they have always assumed . . . that they're entitled and that life should be a bed of roses."

The parents Kindlon interviewed expressed the bewilderment that many parents reveal in the face of today's challenging parenting environment. Almost half said they were less strict than their parents had been. And they too, like the parents in the TIME/CNN poll, pleaded overwhelmingly guilty to indulging their children too much. "It's not just a little ironic," Kindlon writes, "that our success and newfound prosperity—the very accomplishments and good fortune that we so desperately desire to share with our children—put them at risk."

So the job of parenting is harder than ever, parents say they don't think they are doing it very well, and lots of people on the sidelines are inclined to agree. But for all the self-doubt, it is still worth asking: Are today's parents really doing such a terrible job? Are kids today actually turning out so bad?

As far as one can register these things, the evidence actually suggests the opposite. Today's teenagers are twice as likely to do volunteer work as teens 20 years ago, they are drinking less, driving drunk less, having far fewer babies and fewer abortions, and committing considerably less violence. Last year math SAT scores hit a 30-year high, and college-admissions officers talk about how tough the competition is to get into top schools because the applicants are so focused and talented. "We have a great generation of young people right under our noses right now," observes Steven Culbertson, head of Youth Service America, a Washington resource center for volunteering, "and nobody knows it."

Maybe this is some kind of uncanny coincidence, that kids are doing this well despite the way they are being raised rather than because of it. Maybe virtue is their form of adolescent rebellion against parents who indulged every vice. Or it could be that the get-down-on-the-floor, consult-the-child, share-the-power, cushion-the-knocks approach isn't entirely wrong-headed. Perhaps those tendencies have done a lot of good for kids, and what's called for is not a reversal but a step back from extremes.

Certainly that is what many parents are starting to do. "I had one over-the-top birthday party for my child, and I'll never do it again," says Carrie Fisher, daughter of Hollywood star Debbie Reynolds and now the mother of nine-year-old Billie. "She got an elephant, and that's all I'll have to say. It will never happen again. I felt like the biggest ass." Fisher had her epiphany when she heard her daughter bragging to a friend, "My swimming pool is bigger than yours." That prompted some new rules. Among other things, Billie has to clean up her room, a change from Princess Leia's own childhood. "I always thought the fairies did it," she says, laughing. "When I moved into my first apartment, I didn't understand how there were rings in the tub and hair in the sink."

Miami interior decorator Nury Feria, the mother of two teenagers, launched her own little crusade within her job as a designer of children's bedrooms. She was finding herself creating rooms that were more like separate apartments. "Large-screen TVs, computers with individual Internet access, refrigerators, sound systems, video-game centers, leather sofas—the only thing missing was a pool," she says. "I realized that as the designer, I'm also supposed to help shape the lifestyle of the kids, and I didn't like a lot of what I was doing in that regard." So she began subtly trying to guide her clients away from certain amenities, advising some parents to scale back on the queen-size beds for seven-year-old girls or the themed bathrooms that rivaled the Small World ride at Disney World.

Despite incessant requests for a Nintendo system by her twin nine-year-old boys, one mom says she compromises by renting a Nintendo console from Blockbuster a few times a year for $30 each time. "It costs me more to do this, and we could afford to buy it. But I don't want video games in my house all the time. This is our compromise," she says. "My boys are the type to sit there with it all the time."

Dawn Maynard, 44, is a personal trainer and the mother of two boys, 14 and 15. An immigrant from Guyana, she lives in Bethesda, Md., and admits that she spoils her sons with electronics, even though she wishes she didn't. Still, she sees the war being fought all around her and counts the ways she has not surrendered. Some neighbors rented their son a limo to go to the prom. It seated 24.

"My kids are in a county-run math camp that costs less than $200 for the entire three weeks. My sons' best friend is at golf camp for $4,000. I'm always fighting peer pressure with my sons."

All parents have to navigate these social, commercial and psychic pressures; it is how they respond that sets them apart. Many parents talk about this as the great struggle of their households. They find themselves quietly shedding old friends when they diverge over discipline; they shop online to avoid the temptation their kids face up and down the endless aisles; they attend workshops and buy books to help bolster their resolve. If you doubt the guerrilla war, just check in with groups like the Center for a New American Dream: three years ago its website had fewer than 15,000 hits a month; today it gets more than 1.5 million.

Parents joke about looking for other "Amish" parents who will reinforce the messages they are trying to send. "Family dating" is an art form all its own, a feat of social chemistry that makes being 25 and single seem easy. In some circles family dating is still driven by traditional hierarchies of status and class, or off-hours' professional networking, or a shared love of sailing or baseball. But for today's concerned parents, it is increasingly driven by values, by sharing a general worldview on everything from TV watching to candy distribution to curfews. Otherwise, time spent together is just too stressful and explosive.

TIME/CNN Poll

- Are children today more or less spoiled than children 10 or 15 years ago?
  More 80%
  Less 3%
  About the same 15%

- Do children today have to do fewer or more chores?
  Fewer 75%
  More 9%
  About the same 13%

- Are your own children spoiled or not spoiled?*
  Very/somewhat spoiled 68%
  Not very/not at all spoiled 32%

- Are your children exposed to too much advertising when it comes to toys and games they might buy?*
  Too much advertising 71%
  Too little 3%
  About the right amount 25%

From a telephone poll of 1,015 adult Americans taken on July 17–18 for TIME/CNN by Harris Interactive. Sampling error is +/-3.1%.

*Asked of 351 parents. Sampling error is +/- 5.2%.

Of course, families engaged in a rollback still have to live in a world where plenty of other children are overindulged. If you live next door to such a kid, or he's thrown together with yours at school or soccer, it can be a challenge always to be explaining why Johnny gets to have marshmallows for breakfast and your kids don't. But the rules send your kids a message all their own, beyond the fact that marshmallows rot their teeth. The rules are a constant reminder that Mom and Dad care, that the kids' health is important to you, that kids are not home alone. And most of all, that it's O.K. to be different.

Parents who give up and back off leave their children at the mercy of a merciless culture. The ones who stand firm and stay involved often find their families grow closer, their kids stronger from being exposed to the toxins around them and building resistance to them. Ariana Marion ended up getting her car. She graduated with honors in June and heads to Wellesley in the fall. "There's a part of us that says we've still given them too much," says her mother Diane, "that wants to take them to live on a farm for a few years and drive a tractor. But we definitely feel we did the right thing by making her earn the car, by making her wait. And the best thing for us as parents was to learn that she was the kind of girl, and now woman, who could step up to the challenge."

V. Planning Parenthood

Editor's Introduction

Once upon a time, there was only one way to have children—through sexual intercourse—and it normally took place within the confines of marriage. Couples who were unable to have children either adopted or went childless, and those who had children outside of marriage were often looked down upon and forced to live on the fringes of "respectable" society. Today, social mores have changed drastically, and women and men have more choices than ever about when and if they will become parents. Control over biology does not reduce worries, however, as parents (especially women) must face the fact that science can extend childbearing years just so far, and modern methods of artificial reproduction are only available to those who can afford them. These important issues related to parenthood are the subject of Section V.

"The Perils of Early Motherhood" by Isabel V. Sawhill describes the push by conservatives for stronger marriages and fewer divorces. Efforts to increase marriages among low-income individuals (particularly welfare recipients) are aimed at reducing the number of children being raised in single-parent homes. The author contends, however, that preventing early motherhood among those who are not ready for it is as important as increasing marriages among unwed parents. She thinks early marriage will be hard to achieve among most of the population because of the trend toward having children later in life, and that early marriage could prove inconsistent with efforts to promote higher education among America's youth as well as efforts toward long-term marital stability.

"Human in the Age of Mechanical Reproduction" by Karen Wright details the many methods of having a child with the assistance of medical technology. Wright points out some of the problems inherent in the increased use of such artificial methods, including the high cost and risks of using reproductive technology. On the positive side, such methods have allowed groups who would not have been able to have their own biological children in the past (singles, gays and lesbians, and post-menopausal women) to do so.

In "The Ethics of Human Cloning: James Q. Wilson vs. Leon Kass," Wilson and Kass debate the pros and cons of this highly controversial procedure. In Wilson's opinion, the structure of the family in which a child will be raised is more important than how the child arrives there. He points out that other means of having children—such as surrogacy—are equally controversial, and he voices his support for human cloning, if limited to married couples. Kass, on the other hand, fears that cloning will turn childbearing into a business rather than an act of love. He says cloning cannot be compared to other methods of reproduction and believes human beings produced in this way are likely to suffer serious identity crises.

In "Childfree in Toyland," author Christopher Clausen details his decision not to have children and how others who make this choice are still greeted with puzzlement in many sectors of society, particularly when they are married. Although couples are marrying later, having children later, and having fewer children, the decision by married couples not to have children remains somewhat unusual. People who have children or long for them are often baffled by such a resolve, and childless couples and individuals often must defend their choice, which is sometimes mistakenly interpreted as indicating a general dislike for children.

The Perils of Early Motherhood[1]

By Isabel V. Sawhill
The Public Interest, Winter 2002

Conservatives have decided that what ails America is that not enough of us are getting and staying married. They have a point. Not only are fewer people marrying than in the past but, more disturbingly, one out of every three children is born outside of marriage. The life chances of these children are seriously compromised. Far more of them will grow up in poverty, fail in school, and enter adolescence with a propensity to repeat their parents' youthful mistakes. Indeed, as Jonathan Rauch has argued, and the data suggest, marriage is displacing both earnings and race as a source of division in America. Children growing up in a one-parent family are four times as likely to be poor as those growing up in a two-parent family, and those growing up in a single-parent white family are three times more likely to be poor than those growing up in a two-parent black family.

Not all children in single-parent homes are adversely affected, of course, but the odds that they will succeed are considerably lower than for children who grow up in intact families. Moreover, when single-parent families predominate in a community, children grow up with few male role models and do not view marriage as a realistic option. The argument that this gives rise to various forms of antisocial behavior, especially among young men, remains controversial, but it should not be dismissed.

Having successfully reformed the tax system to favor marriage in 2001, conservatives are now targeting the welfare system. They are disappointed that most states have not taken to heart the strong emphasis on marriage and on reducing unwed childbearing in the 1996 federal welfare-reform law, known as Temporary Assistance for Needy Families or TANF. In the round of reform expected in 2002, they want these family formation goals to be given at least as much weight as the goal of moving single mothers into work.

But this raises the question of how best to achieve these goals. Robert Rector of the Heritage Foundation has suggested earmarking 10 percent of all TANF funds (about $1.5 billion per year) for such activities as marriage education and counseling, especially in high-risk communities. Charles Murray has suggested, as an experiment, cutting off all means-tested benefits for unwed mothers under 18 in one state. Governor Frank Keating of Oklahoma is

---

1. Reprinted with permission of the authors from *The Public Interest*, No. 146 (Winter 2002), pp. 74–84 © 2002 by National Affairs, Inc.

emphasizing a reduction in divorce rates. Many in the "fatherhood movement" want more resources devoted to helping young unwed fathers acquire the motivation, skills, and job opportunities that will enable them to marry the mothers of their children—or barring that, at least to be more involved in raising these children. Still others want to target young people who have not yet married or had children in order to prevent unwed births from occurring in the first place. The current welfare-reform law contains a number of provisions intended to reduce nonmarital births. These include a requirement that teen mothers live with their parents or in another supervised setting, bonuses for states that reduce out-of-wedlock childbearing, and funding for abstinence education programs. The law also permits states to deny additional benefits to women who have children while on welfare ("family caps").

These agendas are not necessarily mutually exclusive, but they involve different strategies (encouraging marriage, reducing divorce, discouraging early births) and different target groups (married or romantically involved couples, unwed parents, and young unmarried men and women, including teens). Obviously, marriage is a good thing, but in my view, preventing early childbearing among those who are still young and unmarried is likely to yield the most social benefits, including the restoration of the institution of marriage.

Is Marriage the Solution?

Most people would agree that the ultimate goal is to increase the number of children growing up with two biological, married parents. Reducing divorce rates can contribute to this end. However, after increasing sharply in the 1960s and 1970s, divorce rates have leveled off or even declined modestly since the early 1980s. Moreover, children in divorced families are generally much better off than those born to never-married mothers: They more often retain a relationship with both parents, are more likely to receive support from a nonresident father, and are less likely to receive welfare or other government assistance. Finally, most of the increase in child poverty between 1980 and 1996 was related to the increase in nonmarital childbearing over this period, not to greater divorce. In short, efforts to strengthen marriages in ways that reduce the likelihood of divorce should be welcomed, but divorce rates, though high, are not the crux of the problem and should not be the focus of any new effort.

The real problem is too many unmarried women having babies. Most of these women are very young when they have their first child. While only 30 percent of *all* nonmarital births are to women under the age of 20, half of *first* nonmarital births are to teenagers and most of the rest are to women in their early twenties. So the pattern typically begins in the teenage years or just beyond, and once begun often leads to additional births outside of marriage. There are two solutions to this problem. One is to encourage these young women to marry the fathers of their children (assuming the fathers are willing). The other is to convince them to delay child-bearing until they are older and married.

Most women eventually do marry—90 percent by age 45. The problem is one of timing. Up until their mid twenties, more women have had babies than are or have been mar-ried. Those calling for more marriage are really calling

> *Younger mothers often lack the maturity, patience, and education that a child needs.*

for earlier marriages. But this would reverse a strong and gener-ally healthy trend toward marriage at a later age among both men and women. Between 1960 and 1999, age at first marriage increased from 20 to 25 for women and from 23 to 27 for men. Age at first marriage is one of the strongest predictors of marital stabil-ity. One recent study by Tim Heaton at Brigham Young University based on data from the National Survey of Family Growth finds that almost all of the decline in divorce rates since 1975 is related to the increase in age at first marriage. Not only is this trend good for marriage, it is good for children as well. Younger mothers often lack the maturity, patience, and education that a child needs.

The argument will be made that in earlier times it was common for women to marry young. But our economy now demands much higher levels of education than in earlier periods, and women as well as men have greater opportunities to pursue both education and a career beyond high school. To be sure, some women may want to forego such opportunities in order to become full-time wives and mothers at an early age. But a social policy that actively encourages such early marriage would be inconsistent with one that also favors investments in education and in stable, long-term marriages.

Perhaps what is really intended by marriage advocates is not a set of policies that would encourage earlier marriages across the board but only in cases where a woman is already pregnant or has had a child. Such "shotgun" or "after-the-fact" marriages to the bio-logical father were common in the past but have virtually disap-peared in recent years. Their modern counterpart is what is often called "fragile-family" initiatives—efforts to work with young cou-ples, many of whom are romantically involved or cohabiting at the time of the baby's birth, to form more stable ties and, where appro-priate, to marry. These efforts often involve education, training, counseling, and peer support for the fathers. An evaluation of one such effort, Parents Fair Share, produced somewhat disappointing results. About two-fifths of all out-of-wedlock births are to cohabit-ing couples, and cohabitation seems to be rapidly replacing mar-riage as a preferred living arrangement among the younger generation. These cohabiting families are much less stable than married families. Less than half of them stay together for five years or more. Whether such couples can be persuaded to marry and whether these marriages would endure if they did is not clear, but some research suggests that marriages preceded by cohabitation are less stable than those that are not. In the meantime, any program that provides special supports, such as education and training to unwed parents, whether mothers or fathers, runs the risk of rewarding behavior that society presumably would like to discourage.

> *Once a woman has had a child outside of marriage, her chances of marrying plummet.*

Many unwed mothers cohabit not with the biological father of their children but with another man, and some of these relationships may also end in marriage. But, surprising as it may seem, such stepfamilies seem to be no better for children than being raised in a single-parent home.

The Real Problem

More importantly, once a woman has had a child outside of marriage, her chances of marrying plummet. Daniel Lichter of Ohio State University finds that the likelihood that a woman of a given age, race, and socioeconomic status will be married is 40 percent lower for those who first had a child out of wedlock (and 51 percent lower if we exclude women who marry the biological father within the first six months after the birth). By age 35, only 70 percent of all unwed mothers are married, in contrast to 88 percent among those who have not had a child. Lichter compares women who had a premarital pregnancy terminated by a miscarriage to those who carried to term, and finds that these differences in marriage rates persist. This suggests that the lower rates of marriage are caused by having a baby out of wedlock, rather than simply reflecting the pre-existing characteristics of this group of women. Unwed mothers are less likely to spend time at work or in school where they can meet marriageable men. And having had one child out of wedlock, they appear to be relatively uninhibited about having additional children in the same way. For these or other reasons, early unwed childbearing leads to less marriage and more illegitimacy. Thus a key strategy for bringing back marriage is to prevent the initial birth that makes a single woman less marriageable throughout her adult years.

Not only are unwed mothers less likely to marry than those without children, but when they do marry, they do not marry as well. Their partners are more likely to be high school dropouts or unemployed than the partners of women who have similarly disadvantaged backgrounds but no children. Although marriage improves an unwed mother's chance of escaping from poverty, it does not offset the negative effects associated with an unwed birth, according to Lichter and his colleagues.

My conclusion is that efforts to promote marriage and reduce divorce hold little promise for curbing the growth of single-parent families. What is needed instead is a serious effort to reduce early, out-of-wedlock childbearing—something that, unlike encouraging marriage, we probably can accomplish. Certainly, some of what needs to be done is controversial, but no more so than the promarriage agenda that many conservatives now tout. Indeed, the public consensus in favor of reducing teen pregnancy and early childbearing is strong, whereas support for a promarriage agenda is considerably weaker. Whole segments of the body politic are skeptical of, if not downright opposed to, the marriage agenda. This includes, in addition to many feminists, some conservatives of a libertarian bent for whom this seems like social engineering run amok. Finally, a promarriage agenda is undercut by powerful cultural trends. As Claudia Winkler, managing editor of the *Weekly Standard*, has noted, the effort to restore a marriage culture "is at odds with deep-rooted, centrifugal American values—individualism, pluralism, the separation of church and state—that have never been more vigorous." Of the two means for insuring that more children are born in wedlock—delayed childbearing or earlier marriages—the former is most consistent with these deep-rooted values.

Of course, we should use the bully pulpit to promote marriage, provide premarital education and counseling, and encourage communities, schools, and parents to teach young people about the benefits of marriage. We should also reduce some of the financial disincentives to marriage, especially in low-income communities. Congress acted in 2001 to eliminate the marriage penalty in the tax code, including the large marriage penalty associated with the Earned Income Tax Credit. Many states have liberalized welfare eligibility standards for two-parent families. More could be done, but any meaningful reduction of marriage penalties in income-tested programs carries enormous budgetary costs and is unlikely to significantly affect behavior. Without a strong effort to prevent early childbearing, these other strategies are unlikely to reduce the growth of single-parent families or to improve the economic and social environment of children.

Reducing Early Childbearing

After climbing steadily at almost 1 percentage point per year for over 20 years, the proportion of births outside of marriage ("the nonmarital birth ratio") leveled off after 1994. This development could be related to an increase in marriage, an increase in births to married women, or a decrease in births to unmarried women, but it appears to be primarily due to this last factor. The teenage birth rate (four-fifths of teen births are out of wedlock) has declined since 1991. In fact, if there had been no decline in the teen birth rate, the nonmarital birth ratio would have continued to climb through the late 1990s, though not as rapidly as in the prior decade. More specifically, if teen birth rates had held at the levels reached in the early 1990s, the nonmarital birth ratio would, by 1999, have been more than a percentage point higher. This suggests that a focus on teenagers (although not to the exclusion of women in their early twenties, who also contribute disproportionately to out-of-wedlock births) has a major role to play in reducing both out-of-wedlock childbearing and the growth of single-parent families.

What caused the decline? Can additional steps be taken to lower the rate (and ratio) further? The decline in teen pregnancy rates and births has been driven by both declining rates of sexual activity among teens and better contraception. Proponents of abstinence like to think that the former has been most important, while proponents of birth control give greater weight to changes in contraceptive behavior. From the existing data, it is not possible to determine the precise role of each, but almost everyone agrees that both have been important. There is a growing public consensus that abstinence is preferable, especially for school-age youth, but that contraception should be made available. Polling by the National Campaign to Prevent Teen Pregnancy has consistently found majority support for

---

The decline in teen pregnancy rates and births has been driven by both declining rates of sexual activity among teens and better contraception.

---

this view, with 73 percent of adults agreeing with the proposition that teens should not be sexually active but that if teens are they should have access to contraception. Support for this moderate position has increased 14 percent since 1996.

The emphasis on abstinence, including new funding for abstinence education in the 1996 welfare-reform bill, is helping to reduce teen pregnancies and out-of-wedlock births. Yet evaluations of abstinence education programs have thus far failed to show much evidence of success. How does one explain this discrepancy? In my view, the messages about abstinence are having an impact less because they are embedded in so-called "abstinence only" education programs and more because they have influenced the entire culture, from traditional sex education programs and faith-based efforts, to messages in the media, to the way in which parents communicate with their children. The abstinence message is no longer the exclusive province of a small band of conservative activists. It is now being promoted by many liberal groups and is widely endorsed by most ordinary Americans, including parents, teachers, many political leaders, and to a lesser degree, by teens themselves. This shift in both attitudes and behavior during the 1990s, to which the fear of AIDS and other sexually transmitted diseases contributed, is significant.

The decline in teen pregnancy and birth rates beginning in the early 1990s predates welfare reform. We saw a drop in second or higher-order births to teens who were already mothers in the early 1990s, and this appears to have been caused by the availability for the first time of longer-lasting, more effective forms of contraception such as Depo Provera. These methods are not widely used but have caught on particularly among the subgroup of young women who have already had a baby. But a much sharper decline in births to teens began in the latter half of the 1990s. Evidence suggests that welfare reform, along with more extensive and effective efforts to prevent teen pregnancy, played a large role in producing recent trends.

Messages and Programs

Not only has the teen birth rate declined and the nonmarital birth ratio leveled off, but in the late 1990s the proportion of children living in a single-parent family stabilized or even declined modestly for the first time in many decades. This reversal was most notable for low-income families and for those with less education or very young children, just as one would expect if welfare reform were the cause. Looking at data for 1997 and 1999, for example, Gregory Acs and Sandi Nelson of the Urban Institute found that the share of families composed of single mothers living independently declined almost 3 percentage points more among families in the bottom income quartile than among those in the second quartile.

It would be premature to attribute all or even most of these changes to the 1996 law. Evaluations of some of the provisions, such as family caps, the state illegitimacy bonus, or abstinence education programs, have not shown clear impacts. Arguably, much more important than any of these specific programs are the new messages sent by welfare reform about time limits, work, and abstinence. Young women who decide to have children outside of marriage now know that they will receive much more limited assistance from the government. Young men are getting the message that if they father a child they will be expected to pay child support. The steady, broad messages about work, family formation, sexual abstinence, and the need for fathers to support their children are the key.

These messages have been combined with new efforts on the part of states, communities, and nonprofit (including faith-based) organizations to prevent teen pregnancy. Unfortunately, current efforts, although more extensive than in the past, are fragmented, underfunded, and often ineffective.

The good news is that in the past five years, research on teen pregnancy prevention programs has found that a number are working. Douglas Kirby's review, *Emerging Answers*, published in the summer of 2001, identifies several rigorously evaluated programs that have reduced teen pregnancy rates by as much as one-half. Some effective programs involve teens in community service or afterschool activities with adult supervision and counseling. Others focus more on sex education but not necessarily just on teaching reproductive biology. The most effective sex education programs provide clear messages about the importance of abstaining from sex or using contraception. They teach teens how to deal with peer pressure and how to communicate and negotiate with partners. This research needs to be aggressively disseminated. Since there are a variety of different approaches that can be effective, communities should be allowed to choose the ones that best fit their needs and values.

More emphasis also needs to be placed on the potential of sophisticated media campaigns to change the wider culture. Such campaigns have been used to change a variety of behaviors in the past, but their full potential has not been tapped in the case of pregnancy prevention. Some nonprofit groups, such as the National Campaign to Prevent Teen Pregnancy and the National Fatherhood Initiative, are working in partnership with the media to include new messages in the television shows most often watched by teens. Many states are using the abstinence education funds from the welfare-reform bill for public-service announcements, but additional resources, including some that could be used to design and implement a national effort, are needed.

Social Policy That Works

The reforms instituted in 1996 sent a strong message that women who bear a child outside of marriage will no longer be able to raise that child without working, and that the men who father such children will have to contribute to their support. The early indications are that this message is being heard: Teen birth rates have fallen, the share of children born out of wedlock has leveled off, and the share of young children living in married families has grown. And given time for new social norms to evolve, the effects of reform will likely increase. The goal of increasing marriage is laudable, but pushing tough promarriage policies (such as denying all benefits to young women having children out of wedlock) further would upset the fragile political coalition supporting current reforms.

Our focus must remain on childbearing outside of marriage, not marriage per se. Divorce rates may be high, but they are not increasing and have played no role in the growth of single-parent families for several decades. Most of that growth, and the associated growth in child poverty in the 1980s and early 1990s, was caused by increased childbearing among young, single women. Once such women have had a child, their odds of ever getting married plummet. Many point to the shortage of "marriageable men"—that is, men with good job prospects—in the communities where these women live, but there is a shortage of "marriageable women" as well. Most men are going to think twice about taking on the burden of supporting someone else's child.

If we want to encourage marriage, prevent divorce, and ensure that more children grow up with married parents, we must first insure that more women reach adulthood before they have children. This is a necessary, if not sufficient, condition for success. It implies redoubling efforts to prevent teen pregnancy. And it means convincing young men and women who have not yet had a baby that there is much to lose if they enter parenthood prematurely, and much to gain if they wait until they are married.

Human in the Age of Mechanical Reproduction[2]

BY KAREN WRIGHT
DISCOVER, MAY 1998

"Mommy, where do babies come from?"

Parents have dreaded this question ever since the stork made its first delivery. But today's mommies and daddies have more explaining to do than their own parents could possibly have imagined. Though the birds and bees discussion was never easy, its elements were fairly straightforward: the fireworks exploding, the train chugging through the tunnel, the waves pounding the shore, the occasional reference to anatomy. Once upon a time, baby-making was synonymous with whoopee-making, and frozen eggs were for pastry dough, and seven was how many times you should let the phone ring before you hang up, not how many fetuses you could fit in a womb.

These days, though, the facts of life can sound a lot like science fiction, as late-twentieth-century humanity grapples with the rise of noncoital conception. There are now more than a dozen ways to make a baby, the vast majority of which bypass the antiquated act of sexual congress. The last three decades have seen the advent of such high-tech interventions as fertility drugs, in vitro fertilization, donor eggs, donor sperm, donor embryos, and surrogate mothering. In the works are still more advanced technologies, such as the transfer of cell nuclei, embryo splitting, and even, if at least one man has his way, the cloning of human adults.

These techniques generally are gathered under the heading of "assisted reproduction." All the ones in use today were pioneered for and are usually employed by infertile couples of childbearing age. But they are also used by people with less conventional notions of parenting—singles, postmenopausal women, and gay partners. In the near future, assisted reproduction may become standard procedure for anyone who wants to conceive, and who can afford it. The allure, of course, is control: control over the timing of parenthood, control over "embryo quality," control over genetic disease, control over less pernicious characteristics, such as gender, that are also determined by genes.

So far, owing to federal policy and societal preference, the practice of assisted reproduction is largely unregulated. One specialist has even called it the Wild West of medicine. It's also expensive, bothersome, inefficient, and fraught with ethical complications—but none of those considerations has slowed its growth. Since 1978, when the first test-tube baby was born, the number of fertility clinics in the United States has gone from less than 30 to more than 300. The multibillion-dollar fertility industry has created tens of thousands of babies. Assisted reproduction has relieved the anguish of men and women who, just decades ago, would have had to abandon their hopes of having children. It's also created a world where a dead man can impregnate a stranger, where a woman can rent out her uterus, and where a child can have five parents—and still end up an orphan. It's not at all clear how this new world will change the meaning of family. But it has already transformed what used to be known as the miracle of birth.

Last November an Iowa couple made history, national television, and the covers of *Time* and *Newsweek* when their seven babies were born alive. "We're trusting in God," the McCaugheys told reporters when asked how they would cope with the sudden surfeit of offspring. But to conceive for the second time, Bobbi McCaughey

---

Assisted reproduction has created a world where a dead man can impregnate a stranger, where a woman can rent out her uterus, and where a child can have five parents—and still end up an orphan.

---

had trusted in Metrodin, a fertility drug that stimulates the ripening of eggs in the ovaries. A woman on Metrodin can produce dozens of eggs in a month instead of just one.

Metrodin belongs to a suite of hormones that are used to increase egg development and release, or ovulation. Fertility drugs go by many brand names, like Clomid, Pergonal, Humegon, Fertinex, Follistim, and some have been around for decades. Women who have problems ovulating regularly can often conceive by the time-honored method once fertility drugs have improved their chances of success.

Even so, taking fertility drugs is not like taking aspirin. Most are administered by daily injections that couples are trained to perform. The drugs themselves aren't cheap—a single dose of Fertinex, for example, is about $60—and most doctors monitor the progress of egg ripening with ultrasound scans and blood tests that add to the overall cost. Ultimately, a cycle of treatment with fertility drugs may cost more than $1,500.

And there are risks. The most common is multiple pregnancy: the simultaneous conception of two or (many) more fetuses, like the McCaugheys'. Despite the celebratory atmosphere that greeted the Iowa septuplets, such pregnancies are in fact a grave predicament for would-be parents. Multiple pregnancies increase the odds of maternal complications such as high blood pressure and diabetes. And they pose even greater risks for the unborn. The fetuses gestating in a multiple pregnancy are far more susceptible than their singlet peers to miscarriage, birth defects, low birth weight, and premature birth, as well as lifelong problems that can result from prematurity—including cerebral palsy, blindness, kidney failure, and mental retardation.

There are ways to get around the problem of multiple pregnancy. One is to abstain from sex if ultrasound scans reveal that a plethora of eggs is poised for release. Statistics suggest, however, that many couples choose not to exercise this option. Whereas in the general population the rate of multiple pregnancy is 1 to 2 percent, the rate among women treated with fertility drugs can be as high as 25 percent.

Another way to deal with the risks of multiple pregnancy is to eliminate some fetuses before they are born. Infertility specialists call this technique selective reduction. It is performed before the third month of pregnancy by injecting selected fetuses with potassium chloride, which stops the heart. A doctor inserts a needle through the abdomen or vagina of the mother-to-be to deliver the injection.

Like most techniques of assisted reproduction, selective reduction introduces ethical problems as it solves medical ones. For many couples, the decision of whether and how much to reduce is traumatic. Some, including the McCaugheys, simply refuse to do it. Others accept the agony—and irony—of destroying surplus fetuses as an unfortunate consequence of their condition. Yet still other people feel comfortable enough with the technique to use it for practical, rather than medical, reasons. "There are patients that will push very hard to reduce from three fetuses to two," says Benjamin Younger, executive director of the American Society for Reproductive Medicine. "They'll say, 'Doctor, I can't cope with triplets.'"

If an infertile couple chooses to pursue the more advanced procedures of assisted reproduction, selective reduction is only one of several trials they may face. "I don't think I've ever done anything as difficult," admits a Boston woman who became pregnant after two years of ever-escalating interventions. "You have to really want it."

Kathryn Graven and her husband decided to start a family when Graven was 34. After nine months of trying by the usual route, they went to an area clinic for a fertility workup. There are various causes of infertility, including hormonal imbalance in women, low sperm count in men, and blockages in the reproductive tract of either partner. But tests failed to identify a specific cause for the Gravens', so their doctor recommended conservative treatment. In each of three months, Graven tried the fertility drug Clomid, which is taken orally, to stimulate egg production, followed by artificial insemination with her husband's sperm. When that didn't work,

Graven switched to Fertinex, which is injected beneath the skin. After two rounds of Fertinex and artificial insemination also failed, the couple decided to try in vitro fertilization.

IVF is the cornerstone of assisted reproductive technology. The procedure—in which ripe eggs are removed from the ovaries and incubated with sperm—greatly improves the haphazard gambit of traditional in vivo fertilization. It also introduces another level of complexity and expense. In addition to egg-ripening hormones, a woman undergoing IVF will usually take a protean cocktail of drugs designed to suppress and then trigger the release of mature eggs. Egg retrieval, done by guiding a hollow needle through the wall of the vagina and into the nearby ovaries, is characterized as a minor surgical procedure. ("The next day I felt like a Roto-Rooter had gone through my insides," says Graven.) And then the fertilized embryos have to be transferred back to the uterus.

When Graven's IVF attempt failed as well, her doctor recommended a more advanced technique: gamete intrafallopian transfer, or GIFT. In this procedure, eggs are harvested, mixed with sperm, then returned to the fallopian tubes—where egg and sperm normally meet—to fertilize. GIFT requires a longer and more complicated operation, with three incisions in the patient's abdomen, and about two days' recovery. But the success rates are 5 to 10 percent higher than those of IVF. It worked for Graven: she is to give birth in July, at the age of 37.

GIFT is one of several variations on the IVF theme that were introduced in the 1980s as infertility specialists sought to expand their skills in assisted reproduction. Even with these innovations, however, the efficacy of assisted reproduction is sobering. Graven's experience was typical of what many infertile couples might undergo, except in one respect: Graven got pregnant. Success rates for IVF depend on a patient's age and vary from clinic to clinic and from procedure to procedure. But the ballpark figure—the so-called take-home baby rate—is one live birth for every five IVF cycles. Infertility specialists point out that the success rates for these procedures increase every year and that in any given month a fertile couple's chance of conceiving by traditional means is also one in five. According to the American Society for Reproductive Medicine, more than half of all infertile couples could attain pregnancy if they persisted long enough with treatments for assisted reproduction.

But that also means that about half will never have a baby, no matter how much therapy they get. And one thing about making babies by the usual means is that it's free. If at first you don't succeed you can try, try again, without taking out a second mortgage. A single cycle of IVF, on the other hand, costs between $8,000 and $10,000. Special options like GIFT may cost more. Graven didn't have to pay for most of her treatment, because Massachusetts is one of ten states that mandate insurance coverage for infertility treatment. The bill for her pregnancy would have been well over $25,000.

Is it worth it? The market says yes. Although rates of infertility have remained constant, demand for infertility services has risen steadily in the past two decades. Today about 6 million couples in the United States have fertility problems; half of them go to their doctors for help, and about a quarter end up trying assisted reproduction. Whether those couples view these attempts as a blessing or a curse "depends on the outcome," says Margaret Hollister, director of the help line at RESOLVE, a national infertility support group based in Somerville, Massachusetts. "The treatments are stressful, expensive, and require a big time commitment."

Of course, the same could be said of parenting. The stress associated with infertility, however, may be especially pernicious. Alice Domar, director of the behavioral-medicine program for infertility at Beth Israel Deaconness Medical Center in Boston, has found that women who have been trying to get pregnant via assisted reproduction for two years or more have rates of depression as high as those

---

Infertility patients describing their encounters with assisted reproduction use words like roller-coaster ride, addiction, and obsession.

---

of patients with cancer, heart disease, and AIDS. She also finds that conception rates in severely depressed patients improve when the depression is treated.

Domar has used her results to argue that infertility should be regarded as a serious medical condition and that more research needs to be done on the connection between mind and reproductive machinery. Trouble is, Domar's studies don't ascertain whether her subjects' depression is caused by the trials of infertility per se or by the tribulations of infertility treatments. Infertility patients describing their encounters with assisted reproduction use words like roller-coaster ride, addiction, and obsession. Fertility drugs are renowned for causing moodiness, as well as cramping, weight gain, and bloating. And the demands of tracking ovulation can turn a person's world upside down. During some parts of the cycle, a patient might visit her IVF clinic once or even twice a day for blood tests, ultrasound scans, and injections. "Your life starts revolving around the beginning, middle, and end of your cycle," says Graven. "Monitoring your body becomes a full-time job."

Moreover, pursuing parenthood via assisted reproduction means being confronted with ethical decisions well outside the range of most people's moral radars. Because IVF techniques often give rise to multiple pregnancies, selective reduction is an issue here as well.

Couples undergoing IVF must also decide how many eggs to fertilize and transfer at one time (which bears on the question of multiple pregnancy), whether they want to create and freeze embryos for future use, and what the eventual disposition of any unused frozen embryos should be. Former spouses have waged custody battles over frozen embryos, and in at least one case the attending IVF clinic claimed the embryo as its lawful property. Legally, human embryos occupy a gray area all their own, somewhere between human life and some rarefied form of property.

Assisted reproduction also invites the preselection of embryos based on genetic traits, and all the moral dilemmas that may accrue thereto. Screening is done by removing a single cell from an eight-cell embryo and analyzing the chromosomes or DNA in the cell nucleus. Already some clinics offer to screen in vitro embryos for genes related to cystic fibrosis, hemophilia, and muscular dystrophy. Couples can decide which of the embryos they've created meet their specifications; the rejected embryos can be discarded or donated to research.

Finally, assisted reproduction has opened the door to all manner of gamete swapping and surrogacy, from the simplest and oldest method—artificial insemination with a donor's sperm—to more complex scenarios in which any combination of donor eggs, donor sperm, and donor embryos may be used. In addition to biological surrogate motherhood (the method that created the celebrated Baby M), "gestational surrogates" will agree to carry and give birth to a baby to whom they bear no genetic relation whatsoever. It is now possible for a person to "have" a baby by procuring eggs and sperm from donors and hiring a "birth mother" to do the rest (this has been done). It is possible for a woman to use a birth mother for cosmetic reasons or convenience alone (this has also been done). It is possible for the sperm of dead men to be retrieved and used to impregnate their widows (likewise). It is possible for women long past the age of menopause to give birth (this, too, has already happened).

Another exceptional birth captured headlines last October, when a woman whose ovaries were nonfunctional delivered two healthy boys courtesy of Reproductive Biology Associates in Atlanta. RBA had engineered the twins' conception using donor eggs frozen for more than two years. Because the sheer size and complexity of the human egg make it more susceptible than sperm to damage during freezing, protocols for the cryopreservation of eggs have been difficult to perfect. Until recently, in fact, most attempts at egg freezing have failed. The twins are the first of their kind to be born in the United States.

Though RBA's achievement was quickly overshadowed by the arrival of the Iowa septuplets, the egg-freezing feat has more significant ramifications. Once it becomes widely available, cryopreservation will offer a unique opportunity to women: the chance to store their young eggs for use at a later date. Defects in aging eggs are thought to be responsible for the declining fertility of older women; indeed, donor-egg technology has demonstrated that the rest of the female reproductive apparatus withstands the test of time. By assuring women a lifetime of viable gametes, egg freezing could let them beat the biological clock.

Of course, women would then be using assisted reproduction for their own convenience rather than for treatment of an existing medical condition. In this respect, egg freezing echoes a common theme in assisted reproduction. Current techniques were developed to help patients with specific medical problems—egg freezing, for example, will allow cancer patients whose eggs would be destroyed by radiation to set aside some gametes prior to therapy. Yet inevitably, the fruits of infertility research expand reproductive options for all men and women. And these choices are not always easy to live with, for individuals or for society.

A striking example comes from the laboratory of reproductive endocrinologist Jamie Grifo at New York University Medical Center. In another effort to beat the biological clock, Grifo is transferring the nuclei from older women's eggs into younger eggs from which the nuclei have been removed—that is, enucleated eggs. When these hybrid cells are artificially stimulated to divide, the transferred nuclei don't show the chromosomal abnormalities typical of vintage eggs. Grifo's work is still in the research stage, but he hopes eventually to fertilize such eggs and implant them in his patients.

Grifo is not cloning humans, but his experiments draw on established mammalian cloning technology. Lamb 6LL3, better known as Dolly, was created by nuclear transfer from an adult cell to an enucleated egg. Grifo emphasizes that he's concerned only with transfers between egg cells for the purpose of treating infertility; he says he is strongly opposed to human cloning, and that in any case it will take years for researchers to figure out how to do it. "But the fact is, it's possible," he says. "I just can't think of any clinical indications for it."

If Grifo can't, someone else can. Richard Seed, a physicist turned infertility entrepreneur, made headlines in January when he announced that he was seeking funds to establish a laboratory for the cloning of adult human beings.

The National Bioethics Advisory Commission recommended a ban on human cloning back when Dolly first saw daylight. More recently, President Clinton reiterated his call for a five-year moratorium on human cloning research. But the American Society for Reproductive Medicine, which issues ethical guidelines for the use of assisted-reproduction technologies, has taken the middle ground. "We do not support the cloning of an existing—or previously existing—individual," says Younger. "But that is not to say that cloning technology is bad." Cultures of cloned nerve cells, for example, could be used to treat spinal-cord injuries, he says. "We would not like to see research curtailed."

The society has also come out in favor of continuing research on embryo "twinning"—a procedure, done so far only in animals, in which a single embryo is divided to create two genetically identical individuals. The society's rationale is that the technique of embryo twinning could provide infertile couples with twice as many embryos to implant. But the distinction between cloning and twinning grows obscure if, say, one of the twinned embryos is frozen until its sibling has grown to adulthood.

Critics of assisted reproduction fear that today's innovations will become tomorrow's imperatives. Already some infertile couples feel entrapped by the catalog of choices. "All these technologies, by providing more and more options, make it very difficult to say, 'No, we've tried enough,'" says R. Alta Charo, a law professor at the University of Wisconsin and member of the National Bioethics Advisory Commission. "Choice is not a bad thing—but neither is it an unalloyed good."

And lack of regulation only exacerbates the problems surrounding assisted reproduction. "This field is screaming for regulation, oversight, and control," says Arthur Caplan, a noted bioethicist at the University of Pennsylvania. "What keeps us from doing so is the notion that individuals should have procreative freedom."

Rancor over abortion has also impeded the regulation of technologies for assisted reproduction. Since the 1970s, the United States has outlawed federal funding of research on human embryos or fetal tissue in response to concerns that such research would encourage trafficking in embryos and fetuses. The ban has not been applied to privately funded efforts, however; consequently, most research on assisted reproduction has been conducted beyond the reach of federal regulation and oversight.

> *Critics of assisted reproduction fear that today's innovations will become tomorrow's imperatives.*

Specialists in assisted reproduction, including Grifo, say this is just as well—that regulators wouldn't appreciate the technical and moral complexities of the work. But with the bulk of experimentation going on in private clinics, patients—and their children—can become guinea pigs. Even when couples are not directly involved in experimental procedures, they may be confronted with uncomfortable choices, such as financial incentives to donate their gametes or embryos.

"People often feel compelled by the circumstances—'What else could we do?'" says Barbara Katz Rothman, professor of sociology at Baruch College. "I'm not sure how we should make these decisions, but I'm pretty sure they shouldn't be made by the market."

And market forces affect more than just infertile couples. Although eggs are far more scarce and difficult to obtain than sperm, young women donors are typically given minimal compensation for their time and trouble. But in February the *New York Times* reported that St. Barnabas Medical Center, a fertility clinic in Livingston, New Jersey, has begun offering young women $5,000 to donate eggs—a price reported to be twice that of competitors. Unlike payment for organs, which is illegal, limited payment for eggs is legal. The professional guidelines of the American Society for Reproductive Medicine deem them "body products," not "body parts."

Many observers fear that it is not the participants in assisted reproduction but their children who may suffer most from the imprudent use of these new technologies. For example, with the rising popularity of assisted reproduction, more and more children are being exposed to the risks of premature birth: since 1971 the annual number of multiple births in the United States has more than quadrupled. Scientists and ethicists alike have spoken out against helping single, postmenopausal mothers conceive, arguing that it is morally reprehensible to create children who may well be orphaned. Some question the wisdom of arrangements—like surrogacy or gamete donation—that could diffuse the responsibility of parenthood. And some researchers are concerned with the safety of the procedures themselves for assisted reproduction. A recent—and controversial—Australian study of 420 children suggests that babies produced with the aid of intracytoplasmic sperm injection, in which a single sperm is injected into an incubating egg cell, are twice as likely to suffer major birth defects of the heart, genitals, and digestive tract.

"Everything we do in vitro to a mammalian embryo causes it stress," says Robert Edwards, the specialist who presided over the first test-tube baby 20 years ago. "But there's immense responsibility in the scientific community" to evaluate and eliminate any adverse consequences of new procedures, he says.

Other commentators note that the rights of participants and progeny in assisted reproduction are still undefined. Laws vary widely from state to state on whether a child conceived by donor insemination has the right to know the identity of her biological father. "We never resolved the issues surrounding artificial insemination," says George Annas, a professor of law, medicine, and public health at Boston University. "We just act like we did. And then we import these issues into the new technology."

With the rapid advances in assisted reproduction techniques, the ethical and legal issues can only become more complicated, and the task of resolving them will fall to future generations. But that may be fitting, if it's the children of assisted reproduction who pass judgment on the technology that helped create them.

Thirteen Ways of Looking at a Baby

Since Louise Brown, the first baby conceived outside a human body, was born in England in 1978, techniques for helping infertile couples conceive have mushroomed. It is now possible to have a baby with, say, five parents—the provider of donor egg, the provider of donor sperm, the surrogate mother who undergoes pregnancy, and the two contractual parents. Two of the following methods remain experimental.

Fertility drugs: These drugs stimulate the ripening and release of eggs from the ovary, making conception through intercourse more likely.

Intrauterine insemination: Sperm, either from a partner or a donor, is injected through a catheter into the uterus during ovulation, the period when an egg is released into the fallopian tube.

In vitro fertilization (IVF): Eggs are extracted from the ovaries and mixed with sperm in a petri dish. Once fertilization has occurred, the eggs are incubated for 2 to 3 days. Then the healthiest embryos are inserted into the woman's uterus. She will have been taking hormone supplements to build up the uterine lining for accepting embryo implantation.

Gamete intrafallopian transfer (GIFT): Sperm and eggs are inserted into the fallopian tube in a surgical procedure. Because gametes normally meet in the fallopian tube, GIFT is thought to boost slightly the chances of successful fertilization.

Zygote intrafallopian transfer (ZIFT): Much the same as GIFT except that the egg is fertilized outside the body, then inserted into the fallopian tube as a zygote—an egg that has been fertilized but has not yet begun cell division.

Assisted hatching (AH): The outer membrane, or "shell" of the embryo is punctured to aid implantation in the uterus.

Intracytoplasmic sperm injection (ICSI): A single sperm is injected into an incubating egg cell. Useful in cases where ordinary IVF has failed.

Egg donation: An egg from a donor is fertilized and then implanted into another woman's uterus. This technique can be used for women whose own ovaries are not functioning due to disease or aging—an older woman's uterus has no problem accepting an embryo even when the woman is well past menopause.

Surrogacy: A woman who contracts to undergo a pregnancy for another woman. The baby is conceived with the surrogate's egg and the contractual father's sperm. Alternatively, a couple can transfer an embryo conceived with their own gametes into a surrogate mother's uterus. By this method, a woman for whom pregnancy is impossible or health-threatening can have a biological child.

Embryo donation: A couple receives a surplus embryo from another couple's IVF efforts.

Cytoplasmic transfer: The cytoplasm—the material in a cell that surrounds the nucleus—is extracted from a younger woman's egg and inserted into an older woman's egg. Cytoplasm from a young egg may reduce errors in the genetic material of the older woman's egg, enhancing the chance of successful fertilization.

Egg freezing: One of the most recent—and still experimental—developments, in which eggs are extracted and frozen for years, just as sperm are. Young women could freeze their eggs, then use them at age 35 or more to reduce the risk of creating fetuses with chromosomal abnormalities. Whether most eggs can survive freezing without damage to their DNA is not certain.

Nuclear transfer: This procedure is currently used only in research. The nucleus from an older woman's egg is slipped into a donor egg that has had its nucleus removed. Providing an electrical spark simulates fertilization, and the egg begins the cell division that will allow it to become an embryo. Someday this transfer procedure might facilitate pregnancy in an older woman: after the nucleus from her egg is slipped into a young woman's egg, the egg would be fertilized in normal in vitro fashion and transferred into the older woman's uterus. Creating an offspring from two same-sex parents might also be possible, at least in theory. It is easiest to imagine how this could happen with two men. The nucleus from a body cell from one partner could be slipped into an enucleated donor egg. The other partner's sperm might be able to fertilize that egg, which could then be implanted in a surrogate mother. Whether an egg fertilized in this fashion would survive is not known.

—Sarah Richardson

The Ethics of Human Cloning:
James Q. Wilson vs. Leon Kass[3]

By James Q. Wilson and Leon Kass
American Enterprise, March–April, 1999

James Q. Wilson

"Family structure, not the method of reproduction, is what matters."

Like most people, I instinctively recoil from the idea of cloning human beings. But we ought to pause and identify what in the process is so distressing. My preliminary view is that the central problem is not creating an identical twin but creating it without parents. Children born of a woman—however the conception is produced—will in the great majority of cases enjoy that special irrational affection that has been vital to human upbringings for millennia. If she is married to a man and they, like the great majority of married couples, invest energy, love, and commitment in the child, the child is likely to do well.

My argument is that the structure of the family a child is born into is more important than the sexual process by which the child is produced. If Leon Kass and other opponents of cloning think that sexuality is more important than families, they should object to any form of assisted reproduction that does not involve parental coition. Many such forms now exist. Children are adopted by parents who did not give them birth. Artificial insemination produces children without sexual congress. Some forms of such insemination rely on sperm produced by a man other than the woman's husband, while other forms involve the artificial insemination of a surrogate mother who will relinquish the baby to a married couple. By in vitro fertilization, eggs and sperm can be joined in a Petri dish and then transferred into the woman's uterus.

I have mixed views about assisted reproduction. Some forms I endorse, others I worry about, still others I oppose. The two principles on which my views rest concern, first, the special relationship between infant and mother that is the product of childbirth, however conception was arranged, and second, the great advantage to children that comes from growing up in an intact, two-parent family.

Assisted reproduction, whether by artificial insemination or in vitro fertilization, is now relatively common. In none of those cases is the child the result of marital sex. And in some cases the child is

---

3. Article by James Q. Wilson and Leon Kass from *American Enterprise* March 1999.
Copyright © *American Enterprise*. Reprinted with permission.

not genetically related to at least one parent. I am aware of no study that shows in vitro fertilization to have harmed the children's mental or psychological status or their relationships with parents. A study in England compared children conceived by in vitro fertilization, or by artificial insemination with sperm from an unknown donor, with children who were sexually conceived and grew up in either birth or adoptive families. By every measure of parenting, the children who were the product of either an artificial fertilization or insemination by a donor did better than children who were naturally conceived. The better parenting should not be surprising. Those parents had been struggling to have children; when a new technology made it possible, they were delighted, and that delight motivated them to be especially supportive of their offspring.

Some observers are opposed to all of these arrangements, no matter what their effect on children. Paul Ramsey argued in 1970 that for any third party—say, an egg or sperm donor—to be involved violates the marriage covenant. That is also the view of the Roman Catholic Church. My view is different: If the child is born of a woman who is part of a two-parent family, and both parents work

---

> *The children who were the product of either an artificial fertilization or insemination by a donor did better than children who were naturally conceived.*

---

hard to raise him or her properly, we poor mortals have done all that man and God might expect of us.

Matters become more complex when a surrogate mother is involved. There, a woman is inseminated by a man so that she may bear a child to be given to another couple. That process uses a woman's body from the start for purposes against which her own instincts, as well as our own moral judgments, rebel.

The case of Baby M in New Jersey began with a child born to Mary Beth Whitehead. She had entered into a contractual agreement with William and Elizabeth Stern to deliver the child to them. Mrs. Whitehead had become pregnant through artificial fertilization by Mr. Stern's sperm. After the baby's birth, Mrs. Whitehead refused to surrender it; the Sterns sued. The judge decided that the contract should be honored and the baby should go to the Sterns. On appeal, the New Jersey Supreme Court decided unanimously that the contract was invalid but gave the baby to Mr. Stern and allowed Mrs. Whitehead visiting rights.

The contract, according to the court, was void because it illegally used money to procure a child. More importantly, because no woman can truly give informed consent to relinquishing an infant she has not yet borne and seen, Mrs. Whitehead had not entered into a valid contract. At that time, and so far as I know even today, in every state but Wyoming no woman can agree to allowing her child to be adopted unless that agreement is ratified after birth.

Why, then, did the court give the child to Mr. Stern? The court did not like Mrs. Whitehead. She was poor, ill-educated, moved frequently, received public assistance, and was married to an alcohol abuser. To me, Mrs. Whitehead's condition was largely irrelevant. The central fact was that she was the baby's mother. The overwhelming body of biological and anthropological evidence supports the view that women become deeply attached to their children. The mother-child bond is one of the most powerful in nature and is essential to the existence, to say nothing of the health, of human society.

The child belonged to its mother, period. That does not mean that all forms of surrogate mothering are wrong, but it at least means that the buyer of the surrogate's services is completely at risk. Given that risk, surrogate motherhood will never become popular, but it will occur in some cases.

I favor limiting cloning to intact, heterosexual families and placing sharp restrictions on the source of the eggs. We do not want families planning to have a movie star, basketball player, or high-energy physicist as an offspring. But I confess I am not clear as to how those limits might be drawn, and if no one can solve that puzzle, I would join Kass in banning cloning. Perhaps the best solution is a kind of screened lottery akin to what doctors performing in vitro fertilization now do with donated sperm. One can match his race or ethnicity and even select a sex, but beyond that he takes his chances.

I am persuaded that if only married couples can clone, and if we sharply limit the sources of the embryo they can implant in the woman, cloning will be quite rare. Sex is more fun than cloning, and artificial insemination and in vitro fertilization preserve the element of genetic chance that most people, I think, favor. Dr. Kass is right to stress the mystery and uncertainty of sexual union. That is why hardly any woman with a fertile husband who could obtain sperm from a donor bank will do so. Procreation is a delight.

Leon Kass

"Cloning turns procreation into manufacture."

Wilson begins, as I do, with repugnance. He acknowledges his own instinctive recoil from the idea of human cloning but does not quite trust his sense of moral disquiet, and sets out to reason it away. That places the burden of proof on those who object to cloning rather than on the proponents. Worse, it requires that the reasons offered be finally acceptable to utilitarians who measure only in terms of tangible harms and benefits but who are generally blind to the deeper meanings of things.

Wilson uses the social acceptance of in vitro fertilization to rebut objections against laboratory conception of human life. But by removing human conception from the human body and by introducing new partners in reproduction (scientists and physicians), in vitro fertilization did more than supply what one or both bodies lack to produce an infant. By putting the origin of human life literally in human hands, it began a process that would lead, in practice, to the increasing technical mastery of human generation and, in thought, to the continuing erosion of respect for the mystery of sexuality and human renewal. The very existence of in vitro fertilization, notwithstanding its real benefits, becomes a justification for the next steps in turning procreation into manufacture. The arrival of cloning, far from gaining legitimacy from the precedent of in vitro fertilization, should instead awaken those who previously saw no difficulty with starting human life in Petri dishes.

> *In the event of a divorce, will mommy still love the clone of daddy?*

Wilson does profess sympathy with those who think cloning is contrary to nature, but nature's normative pointings have become invisible to him. Here is probably the biggest philosophical reason for our difference.

At the center of my objection to cloning is my belief in the profundity of sex. At the center of Wilson's is the concern that all children have parents. But the fact is we will be increasingly incapable of defending the institution of marriage and the two-parent family if we are indifferent to its natural grounding in sex. Can we ensure that all children will have two parents if we ignore the natural sexual foundations of parenthood?

Cloning is asexual reproduction. A clone is the twin rather than the offspring of its "source." It has no parents, biologically speaking, unless its "parents" are the mother and father of the person from whom it was cloned.

Wilson is willing to define motherhood solely by the act of giving birth. And if the clone's birth mother is married, her husband will be, by (social) definition, its father. In that way Wilson tries to give a virtually normal biparental identity to this radically aparental child, but in doing so Wilson clings to nature and the natural facts of gestation and parturition as his anchor. For that reason he argues elsewhere for a ban on the laboratory growth of a "newborn" child from sperm to term: "Without human birth, the parents' attitude toward the infant would be deeply compromised."

By playing down cloning's psychological problems of identity and individuality, Wilson is able to treat it as an innocent prospect. But there are unique dangers in mixing the twin relationship with the parent-child relationship. Virtually no parent is going to be able to treat a clone of himself or herself as one does a child generated by the lottery of sex. The new life will constantly be scrutinized in relation to that of the older copy. Even where undue parental expectations on the clone (say, to live the same life, only without its errors) are avoided, the child is likely to be ever a curiosity. Moreover, clones, because they are the flesh and blood (and the look-alike) of only one parent, are likely to be especially implicated in tensions between the parents. In the event of a divorce, will mommy still love the clone of daddy?

Wilson is also naive in believing that cloning can be confined to married couples seeking a remedy for childlessness. In vitro fertilization has not been so restricted; single women now regularly use artificial insemination with donor sperm. Commercial sperm banks are thriving, including those that specialize in eugenics (by providing only sperm from "geniuses"). Couples interested in cloning, especially those who have figured out the dangers of self-cloning, will certainly want to make use of "high-class" donor nuclei. Cloning provides the powerful opening salvo in the campaign to exercise control over the quality of offspring. The dangerous attitude that sees children as products for manipulation rather than gifts to be treasured will be further accelerated.

Given the fracture of the once-respected and solid bonds among sex, love, procreation, and stable marriage, and the relentless march of technology, it will prove impossible to preserve Wilson's faint hopes for limiting cloning to the sphere of traditional parenthood and family life. The right to reproduce (or not) is now widely regarded as a right belonging to individuals: Who are Wilson and I to stand in the way of any unmarried woman's desire for personal fulfillment through motherhood of a clone?

The right to reproduce is also being expanded to include a right to the type of child one wishes. Parents already exercise some choice, through genetic screening, over the quality of their children. Strange requests are already being voiced. Lobbyists for the congenitally deaf are seeking to abort non-deaf fetuses as part of their campaign to "normalize" deafness and to provide only deaf children for the deaf. Gay rights organizations urged the National Bioethics Advisory Commission to declare in favor of cloning. Some advocates even argued that, should homosexuality be shown to have a genetic basis, homosexuals would have an obligation to reproduce through cloning to preserve their kind!

Even if human cloning is rarely undertaken, a society in which it is tolerated is no longer the same society—any more than is a society that permits incest or cannibalism or slavery on even a small scale. It is a society that has forgotten how to shudder, that rationalizes away the abominable. A society that allows cloning has, whether it knows it or not, tacitly said yes to converting procreation into fabrication, and to treating our children as pure projects of our will.

Childfree in Toyland[4]

BY CHRISTOPHER CLAUSEN
THE AMERICAN SCHOLAR, WINTER 2002

On the threshold of thirty and divorce, the personable daughter of a Southern Baptist minister once informed me calmly that any child of hers would probably be a battered child. She was being neither neurotic nor more self-centered than people usually are, merely honest about her strong preference not to have children. The feminist movement was just starting to make such a choice respectable in places where it had influence, which included universities like the one in which we both held temporary jobs. Nonetheless, most of her friends had built their nests and were furnishing them with babies. Her parents, like most, were eager for grandchildren. Determined to be the hero of her own life, what their daughter wanted instead was a Ph.D. and a career. Quite apart from professional ambitions, temperamentally she was one of those people for whom parenthood is an alien role. Her dramatic way of describing her feelings, to a man whose own marriage had recently ended because his wife wanted a child and he didn't, may have been an expression of how inexpressible they were in other circles of her life.

That was in the early 1970s. Since then, life and attitudes are widely assumed to have changed beyond recognition. More than half of married and unmarried women alike now work outside the home. Birth control has improved dramatically. In intellectual circles the phrase "family values" has become a term of ridicule, while "reproductive rights," like "choice," is an accepted synonym for legal abortion. In fact, the story told above seems almost too good to be true, though it is true. It seems to confirm a fashionable academic and journalistic stereotype of dramatic conflict in American society: the religious right versus women's freedom to have professional careers or to determine their own reproductive futures. An array of newspaper articles in the wake of the 2000 census pointed out, sometimes with alarm about an aging society, that the number of temporarily or permanently childless adults has been rising significantly since the seventies. One implication was that, except in the most benighted company, nobody today needs to feel defensive about being "childfree," a term used since the late 1980s by advocates for the rights of non-parents.

The truth is a lot messier, or at least harder to decipher, and has little to do with any ideology. As is usual in controversies about social trends, a variety of sometimes ambiguous statistics fly back

4. Reprinted from *The American Scholar*, Volume 71, Number 1, Winter 2002. Copyright © 2002 by the author. By permission of the publisher.

and forth as ammunition. Perhaps the most helpful are a series issued by the National Center for Health Statistics that display by age cohort the percentage of American women who have never had at least one live birth. In 1998, the percentage of women in the oldest cohort, aged from forty to forty-four, who had never given birth was 16.5. (Almost no women give birth to a first child after their early forties.) With some fluctuations, the proportion of childless women in this age group declines as one goes back in time. In 1970, the earliest year with fully comparable figures, the percentage was 10.6.

This succession of numbers, however, may be interpreted in at least two ways. Enthusiasts for the childfree state, or observers frightened by its implications, can point out that the childless percentage among women who had reached their forties increased by more than half in twenty-eight years. The proportion who had never given birth grew even faster among women who were still in their twenties and thirties. But those who doubt that things have changed radically can note with equal justice that the vast majority of women—more than 80 percent—continue to have children,

---

"You're supposed to have the career, you're supposed to have the guy, you're supposed not to wait to have babies—and you're supposed to do it all really well and look really good while you're doing it."
—**Jennifer Weiner, novelist.**

---

and that the childless percentage in all age groups seemed to level off by the mid-1990s. In its September 2000 report on the fertility of American women, the Census Bureau states that "childless levels are approximately the same now as they were a century ago." While both sexes marry later and have fewer children on the average than they did during the baby boom (if not later or fewer than during the Depression), the question of whether to have any children at all continues to be answered resoundingly in the affirmative.

Despite women's enormously larger participation in careers, despite the almost universal availability of reliable birth control, despite a solid generation of feminists assuring women that reproduction is a matter of choice, despite more than three decades of warnings about overpopulation and environmental degradation, despite the huge contemporary emphasis on personal freedom and self-gratification, despite the manifest economic advantages of childlessness—despite all these influences, having children is still overwhelmingly the norm. As the novelist Jennifer Weiner recently put it, "You're supposed to have the career, you're sup-

posed to have the guy, you're supposed not to wait to have babies—
and you're supposed to do it all really well and look really good
while you're doing it." What has actually declined most strikingly is
not the number of people who choose to have children but the link
between childbearing and marriage. Although nearly nine out of ten
Americans eventually marry at least once, the proportion of children who are born to unwed mothers now exceeds 30 percent and
constitutes the most important cause of child poverty.

Like parenthood itself, the sentimentalizing of childhood that
began with the Romantics some two hundred years ago shows no
signs of decline in public or private life. Since the 1980s, children
have become a justification for every kind of political proposal or
government initiative, from regulating tobacco and HMOs to enact-
ing campaign-finance reform to saving Social Security. In a famous
flight of White House rhetoric from the mid-1990s, President Clinton announced, following an agreement to retarget Russia's ballistic
arsenal, that no American child now had nuclear missiles aimed at
him or her. Education has been the most popular issue in recent
elections, just as "Leave no child behind" was the most widely
quoted slogan of the 2000 campaign. Displayable children have
become an almost mandatory prop for a successful candidate. Child
tax credits are the most popular form of tax reduction. During the
past decade any number of organizations, ranging from the Presby-
terian Church to the state of South Carolina, have proclaimed various twelvemonth periods the Year of the Child. Walt Disney World
is America's most popular tourist destination. "Adult language" now
means profanity; an adult community is a housing development for
the aged. When a singles group demanded during the 2000 presi-
dential campaign that government and other institutions pay more
attention to the needs of childless grown-ups, they were ridiculed in
the press and ignored by candidates.

One strong criticism of the childfree position came from Amitai
Etzioni, a well known social theorist who is the leading figure in the
communitarian movement. Writing in *USA Today*, Etzioni declared:
"One may be tempted to treat this attempt to imitate social move-
ments that address serious social grievances as a poor joke. However, growing work pressures and the high costs of raising children
already discourage many people from having children. Middle-class
people are getting married later and are having fewer children as it
is." Etzioni saw the declining birthrate as a threat to the whole society's future economic well-being, and he recommended that rather
than cut back on what he described as "the meager benefits our society does provide parents," we should consider imitating France by
offering bonuses to encourage Americans to have more children.
Like most cheerleaders for childbearing, Etzioni emphasized that
the benefits to society were not his primary motive. Few people have
children out of a sense of civic duty. "As the childless by choice have
doubtless heard before," this father of five declared, "the reason children are recommended—whether homemade or adopted—is that

most of them turn out to be an unmatchable source of profound joy and deep pride. . . . Quite simply, I am sorry for those who swear off children."

Etzioni is a writer whom I respect and often agree with on other issues. By no stretch of the ideological imagination can he be described as a family-values traditionalist, let alone an ogre of the religious right. If a mainstream, moderate thinker writes this way, where are those who decide against becoming parents to look for moral support? And Etzioni's attitude is by no means unusual. Even on university faculties, people with children frequently still explain to any childless friend over the age of twenty-five, with a varying mixture of envy, flattery, and reproach, that not having children is selfish; that someone as smart as you are should pass his genes along to the future; that such a wonderful person would make an especially wonderful parent; that a clinic could probably help. . . . As in other professions, the prevailing model today is having it all even if it means that the parents never sleep and the kids spend their early lives in day care. Female graduate students in my classes worry loudly and seriously about when the best time

---

The prevailing model today is having it all even if it means that the parents never sleep and the kids spend their early lives in day care.

---

would be to "start a family." Before or after the Ph.D.? After or before tenure? But you might be forty by then.

The biological clock seems immune to deconstruction. That clock's peremptory ticking, like mortality itself, seems to be one of those rhythms that unite the generations rather than divide them. Alarmist media stories on childless professional couples alternate with inspirational features about gentle, enlightened fathers who stay home to change the diapers while their wives earn millions as trial lawyers or investment bankers. The willed-childlessness alternative may be easier in some ways than it was thirty years ago, but its status in most quarters is much closer to uneasy tolerance than full acceptance.

Why we do or don't have children, now that most of us have a choice, is one of the most fascinating questions anyone can ask about human nature. To write on it is to write about oneself, whether overtly or by implication. In fifty-nine years of life I've changed my mind about a great many things, but becoming a father was not one of them. Maybe it was the result of being the oldest of four sons and having my fill of babies early in life. Or maybe not; many eldest children of large families happily rear happy children of their own. In any event, I can recall shyly confiding to my father long before puberty that I thought I would probably not choose to be a parent myself. His response was that when I grew older, I would want to perform the activity that led to the birth of children, and life would take its natural course. I doubted the last part. There was no single issue that led me at an early age to such an independent decision, certainly not a dislike of children, but I already felt sure that having them was for other people.

Among my own parents' closest friends were a brilliant and entertaining couple. The man, a sociologist, had been my father's student at Cornell a decade earlier. When I asked my mother—even more shyly this time—some years after their marriage when they were going to have children, she shook her head and answered that she was afraid they never would. They liked their freedom too much. Although the man was subordinate to my father at the National Institutes of Health, the couple inhabited a cavernous eighteenth-century house in Georgetown instead of, like us, a suburban three-bedroom in Bethesda. They had no need to worry about local schools or playgrounds. They took trips to New York whenever they wanted, and occasionally to Europe. They frequently ate in restaurants. After a few years the woman decided to go to law school. This couple, whose way of life seemed so self-indulgent and immature to my parents, quickly became my closest adult friends and marital ideal.

College was an altogether different experience. There, virtually all my friends of both sexes, regardless of career ambitions, looked forward to parenthood as a matter of course. At the age of twenty I was a naively romantic youth who believed in commitment, devotion, marriage—in other words, with one exception I was utterly conventional when it came to personal life. The exception, which seemed a small thing at the time, was merely the conviction that love and marriage were logically as well as practically separable from parenthood. By the time I graduated, the birth-control pill had come on the market. Two people who were well matched could find a plethora of interesting ways to occupy their time; they had no need for a third or a fourth or a fifth person. I never doubted that children could be a joy and satisfaction to parents who welcomed them into the world with enthusiasm, but my tastes were different. There was certainly no public reason or duty to replace oneself. In 1964 it was already plain that the world was never likely to suffer from under-population.

Getting married prematurely to a bright, lovable fellow student on the assumption that one of us would change our mind over the course of time was an almost inevitable mistake. *Eventually* has a way of becoming *soon*; *soon* eventually becomes *now*. Because it was not a subject on which I had ever experienced inner conflict, I thought very little about the matter until the woman in question began to hear her biological clock ticking louder and more resentfully with every passing year.

I was sadder, wiser, and luckier a decade later when I met the fourth daughter of a Latin teacher and a retired Navy officer. Although we found ourselves in instant accord on the question of parenthood—together with strong feelings about fidelity in the Age of Aquarius, that was one of the early bonds of temperament between us—our own parents could never quite believe it. Each of them had conscientiously reared four apparently sound, healthy offspring and ended up with only three grandchildren. Half their children never reproduced at all. When my mother, by now an urbane feminist who lived in Berkeley, California, got together with my conservative Southern mother-in-law, the one issue on which *they* were in perfect accord was the unfairness of having gone to so much trouble for such a meager return.

My oldest brother died of cancer in his mid-forties, leaving a widow and a son of eight. In the long aftermath, my wife and I happily assumed responsibility for our nephew two or three times a year and gave his mother a break from single parenthood. We did most of the predictable things—took him to restaurants and museums, played baseball, read to him until he got too old, indulged his tastes in food and television, assembled a fiendishly complicated model of Fenway Park, explained the defects of the two-party system, talked to him about his father, made sure he went to bed on time. For days or weeks at a stretch it was a delight to become the quasi-parents of a lively, brainy, exceptionally well-mannered kid, after which we were ready to return him to the everyday responsibility of his mother. As he approached college age, the routine evolved into something solider—less a matter of substituting for someone who has been lost than a bond among people who share indelible memories, interests, and affections.

A lesson the childfree learn early in adult life is that when a friend or sibling asks accusingly why you haven't had children yet, there is only one effective answer. "If I could be sure of getting one just like yours, I'd do it in a minute" is guaranteed to deflect the attack and change the subject. Most people prefer flattery to imitation. Alas, it seldom works with your own parents. On one occasion my father, always an outspoken man, took my wife aside and blurted experimentally, "Chris should have given you a child." To which she responded: "I would have given it right back." My parents never raised the question again, but after Nancy and I had been married twenty years, my mother-in-law was still asking her youngest daughter when she planned to start having a family.

While some men hear biological clocks too, the overwhelming majority of writers on childlessness are women. But it would be a mistake to assume that women who write on the subject, even those who are liberals and feminists, necessarily support the "childfree" position, or for that matter understand it. They may instead, like Stephanie Mencimer, an editor of *Washington Monthly*, complain that women are having fewer children because of the limited government benefits to which Etzioni alluded. In

"The Baby Boycott," Mencimer sneers at the possibility that some women might feel liberated by the prospect of not having children. (What men feel about it is not among her concerns.) "The idea that mass childlessness is the product of a 'lifestyle choice' or a political movement defies common sense. We are, after all, highly evolved primates. Reproductive instincts are hard wired in our brains, and historically, only events of serious magnitude—wars, depressions, famine, and seismic shifts in the economic system, such as the industrial revolution—have caused large numbers of women to forgo having children."

While conceding that a lower birthrate may be good for the environment, she announces: "America's disappearing children are the canaries in our coal mines, a warning that our social and economic system is seriously out of whack." What women typically want, says Mencimer, echoing many other feminists, is both careers and children. Any situation that denies them either is oppressive. The solution is to imitate Sweden, which experienced declining fertility rates and the prospect of a labor shortage in the early 1980s. "Rather than try coercive measures to increase birth rates (like banning abortion or restricting women's educational options) or massive immigration, Sweden chose to make the workplace more accommodating for parents. Swedish women are now guaranteed a year of paid leave after having a baby, the right to work six-hour days with full benefits until their child is in grade school, and subsidized child care." The result is that the birthrate in Sweden rose, though ironically only to the current American level. American women, Mencimer thinks, should put their foot down, so to speak, and refuse to have any babies at all until similar policies are enacted here. Once that happens, men and women alike will return cheerfully to the instinctual pleasures of multiple progeny.

Given this sort of commentary from quarters that might be expected to show sympathy, it is hardly astonishing that the tone of "childfree" publications and Internet sites tends toward extreme defensiveness. Such recent books as Madelyn Cain's *The Childless Revolution* and Laura Carroll's *Families of Two* argue passionately, as their titles suggest, that not having children is quite all right, indeed has become a major trend. Susan Jeffers's evocatively named *I'm Okay, You're a Brat* describes the burdens of being a parent in terms calculated to discourage all but the most determined. Childlessness seems an even more embattled cause on the Web, where its defenders huddle together for comfort and carry on what seem in many cases to be arguments begun long ago with their parents. The sixty-six sites currently listed on the Web's ChildFree Ring constitute an electronic support group with such titles as "No Kidding," "Free at Last," and "Childfree—It's a Choice."

Childfree Families, an advocacy organization whose motto is "You *always* have a choice," announces on its site: "There's an enormous pressure in America to follow a presumed 'typical' path: grow up, get married, and have children. The problem is, not all people really have an interest in having children, and many people realize that they're not well-suited to parenting. We feel that the choice not to have children is and should be a legitimate and respected choice." Under its "mission" statement, Childfree Families repeats the same point even more forcefully: "There's a website for the child-free because there's a need to get the word out: you do not have to have children. You do not have to want children. You don't. And it's perfectly OK." This slightly desperate, coming-out-of-the-closet tone finds an echo at Childfree.net, which makes the same point: "Why a website? Because being childfree-by-choice is rather frowned upon by our kidcentric society, finding information (or links to information) is difficult. . . . We feel like freaks and don't realize exactly how many of us and exactly how much information is out there."

Childfree, a site belonging to a Missouri woman who has been married for ten years and is pursuing a graduate degree in sociology, goes into more detail: "Regardless of how you come to decide not to have children, you are likely to be thought selfish and immature by many of your friends and family. Perhaps we are a little selfish. But many of those people who think we are selfish simply cannot (or will not) accept our position. They are too entrenched in the pronatalism of our society to see anything else. And they are so vocal, sometimes we cannot hear the voices more like our own." The proprietor of Perspective on Children, an Illinois man in his mid-thirties, is seeking a born-again Christian woman to marry who "must be willing to never have or raise children." "It is not surprising," he adds philosophically, "that, as of this writing, I am alone."

> *Not all people really have an interest in having children, and many people realize that they're not well-suited to parenting.*

Some of these authors clearly loathe children. Others take pleasure in nieces, nephews, and the children of friends. But they all feel estranged from what they perceive as a child-centered society. Perhaps the most abjectly beleaguered childfree site belongs to the British Organisation of Non-parents. For reasons that are obscure, Britain, one of the most densely populated countries in the world, seems even more intolerant of intentional childlessness than the comparatively wide-open United States. Anticipating scorn and abuse, the Web site opens with a preemptive strike: "BON is not a bunch of selfish, feckless, child-hating sociopaths, but simply a group of people from all kinds of backgrounds and all walks of life who have decided for various reasons that we do not want children, and who believe that that *choice* should be ours, and anyone else's, to make, free of any stigma, prejudice or pressure from other people." As if this declaration were not sufficiently disarming, the site goes on: "We do not claim that either non-parents or parents are in any way 'better' than the other or any more or less selfish, but we do wish to see non-parents accepted as *different but equal*." In one more display of live-and-let-live good faith, BON announces up front that its adherents have no objection to paying taxes to subsidize family benefits and social services for other people's children.

Although the Bible presents childbearing as part of God's punishment for the sin of Eve, literature offers few encouraging models for the non-celibate childfree. The best-known childless couple in English literature are the Macbeths. Moreover, unless one counts stepmothers, uncles without children of their own win the prize for the most unappealing fictional relatives. Many are outright villains—consider Hamlet's uncle Claudius or the most notorious uncle of them all, Ebenezer Scrooge. Others are simply ineffectual, usually with a comical hint of sexlessness: Dickens's Uncle Pumblechook; Maupassant's Uncle Jules; Faulkner's Uncle Buck and Uncle Buddy, unworldly indistinguishable bachelors, one of whom marries late against his will and produces an even more helpless son, Ike McCaslin, who in turn becomes "uncle to half a county and father to no one." Aunts fare a little better—a self-respecting woman could probably tolerate being compared with Auntie Mame, or at a later age with David Copperfield's Aunt Betsy Trotwood. On the other hand, Fanny Price's Aunt Norris, in *Mansfield Park*, is the most unambiguously evil character in all the novels of Jane Austen, a writer who notoriously did not care for children.

Choosing not to become a parent means refusing to do something that each of one's ancestors has done all the way back to the invention of sexual reproduction. An elderly Englishwoman who is a dear friend of mine thinks any woman who passes up having children is "against life" (adding in the next breath that a man who never fights in a war has likewise missed out on his destiny). Taking this step as an act of will still requires determination, and not only for women. One is both violating unanimous family tradition and resisting a clear if mostly unvoiced consensus in contemporary society, however secular and liberated the immediate environment may be. An almost unchallenged emphasis on children and family is by no means confined to the bromides of politics and religion. Since the 1960s, in the toyland of popular culture, the tastes, interests, and clothing styles of children and adolescents have become norms for anyone who wants to avoid seeming antisocial or over the hill.

Why does a society whose members have so many opportunities continue to place such emphasis on reproduction and its fruits? The British sociobiologist Richard Dawkins maintains that human beings, like other organisms, are simply mechanisms contrived by genes to replicate themselves. For the "selfish gene," success in life means producing as many surviving offspring as possible. According to this theory, we are indeed hardwired to have children. Few social scientists accept this kind of all-or-nothing evolutionary explanation for human behavior. At the same time, few have studied parents' reasons for having children in much depth, perhaps because other explanations usually end up being speculative, vague, or both.

A 1997 article by Robert Schoen et al. titled "Why Do Americans Want Children?" examined the professional literature on the subject and noted gloomily that "there is no explanation for why Americans still want children." Looked at from the purely economic standpoint, the benefits that children provided in an agricultural society "virtually disappear" with the transition to an industrial and post-industrial world. After pointing out that "intended childlessness is still uncommon," however, the study's authors could do no better than to conclude: "Childbearing is purposeful behavior that creates and reinforces the most important and most enduring social bonds. We find that children are not seen as consumer durables; they are seen as the threads from which the tapestry of life is woven."

What really needs explaining, according to most researchers, is why a minority deviates from the norm by choosing *not* to become parents. If Etzioni's and Mencimer's conclusions seem farfetched—after all, the birthrate was at its highest during periods when virtually no government benefits existed for parents or children—others are available, most of them economic. One familiar theory holds that the higher a woman's educational attainment and potential earnings, the greater the "opportunity cost" of having children. By the same token, however, affluent families can afford children more easily than poorer ones, so that the two effects mostly cancel each other out. The more education a woman has, the later she is likely to start bearing children and the fewer she is likely to have, though women's career goals in themselves seem to lack much impact on decisions about having children.

At bottom, according to a 1999 article by Tim Heaton et al., "Persistence and Change in Decisions to Remain Childless," "the relationship between socioeconomic characteristics and childlessness is not strong." Probably to no one's surprise, "Why Do Americans Want Children?" concludes that "childbearing is most likely to occur among traditional homemakers and happily married couples." Black Americans are more likely to have children than whites, to have them earlier, and to have them out of wedlock. Most significantly, maybe, the 1999 study found that "the decision about childbearing appears to be less firm than in previous generations. . . . Few early childbearing intentions appear to be hard and firm." One factor that seems to harden them, ironically, is war. In the wake of September 11, 2001, *New York* magazine published an article called "Baby Talk," which quotes a string of women in their twenties and thirties who suddenly can't wait to have children. "I know three people who told me they wanted to conceive on the day of the attacks," says one. "I totally felt a deep, primal need." Another adds: "After it happened, all those families were out walking around and it made me realize how much I wanted to reproduce. I told my fiancé, 'I'm having *major* baby pangs.'" No one who remembers that the baby boom immediately followed World War II should be surprised.

In a few months I plan to attend the wedding of one of my favorite graduate students and his girlfriend, who is finishing her own Ph.D. in industrial engineering. He is thirty, she twenty-six. Without quite being sure why, they decided long ago not to have children. As the wedding approaches they feel pressure to change their minds, not only from their Catholic parents but from some of their closest contemporaries. They were the main inspiration for this essay, and they would like to see it end with an impassioned statement of the arguments for their position—overpopulation, the environment, and, above all, the right of adults to choose their destinies free from the prejudices of the tribe. Yet there is hardly any issue on which argument is more futile. The motivations on both sides are too deep and obscure. What I would prefer to say to them instead, therefore, goes something like this:

Having or not having children is one of the momentous, irrevocable choices of human life, and those who know from an early age which alternative will make them happier are extremely fortunate. No doubt economic and demographic explanations for fluctuations in the birthrate have a certain statistical validity. They neatly account for its fall during the Depression and, to a lesser extent, during recent decades, when so many women have been pursuing careers. But on the basic question of whether to reproduce, they seem hopelessly shallow. Most people fundamentally want to have children and do, almost regardless of circumstances, while a significant minority prefers not to and sees no good reason why it should. Though they may share the same house, each finds the other a mystery. Not everyone is wired the same way.

But why should we be? In ethical terms, neither alternative is inherently less or more selfish than the other; the one altruistic course would be to adopt a child who has no home. The only adults who deserve special sympathy in this intimate civil war are the undecided, the wavering, the conflicted, who depressingly often either jump too soon into parenthood or leave it until too late, regretting in the end whichever choice they finally made.

VI. Nontraditional
Families

Editor's Introduction

Although the nuclear family remains an important part of American society, other family structures are becoming more widely accepted. Gays and lesbians have made great strides towards acceptance as parents, and single parents and interracial and interethnic couples no longer raise eyebrows. Nevertheless, homosexuals still struggle to be treated with respect as parents, while racially mixed families continue to face unique challenges. Section VI explores these nontraditional families that force Americans to confront received notions of what a family is and should be.

"The Battle to Be a Parent" by Richard Tate relates the case of Paul Washington, Jr., who raised his nephew with his gay partner until the boy was 10. At that point Washington's father sought custody of the child because the boy's grandfather was uncomfortable with the two men's sexuality. As Tate explains, the larger issue of the rights of homosexual parents is particularly contentious when they are not the biological parents of the child in question. While there are ways to establish legal guardianship in such cases, these methods are often quite expensive. Most courts no longer consider sexual orientation alone a reason to terminate parental rights, but gays and lesbians still face many hurdles that heterosexuals do not in this area.

Ta-Nehisi Coates describes the challenges of being the primary caregiver for his young son and how the normal challenges of a single parent are exacerbated by the prejudice he encounters as a black man, in "Confessions of a Black Mr. Mom." Coates, who lives with but is not married to his son's mother, discusses the epidemic of absent fathers in the African American community and talks about efforts within that community to promote responsible parenting by men. He praises calls for both men and women to be responsible for their children, but argues that traditional gender roles in which men are breadwinners and women caregivers and nurturers are outdated.

America has always been proud of its identity as a "melting pot," a distinction that has gained prominence in the last couple of decades as interracial marriages have become more prevalent and more socially acceptable. This growing number of interracial and interethnic marriages is the subject of Lynette Clemetson's article, "Love Without Borders." As Clemetson reports, even in a nation that is supposed to be accepting of all races and cultures, couples who intermarry face a variety of challenges, from dealing with discrimination and racism to blending different cultural backgrounds in the home.

Terry Golway considers the future of the American family in an article titled "The End of the Family?" Golway concedes that many single parents do an admirable job of raising their children and that some parents are better off without their former partners. While there is a growing acceptance of such families in American society, Golway asserts that a two-parent home is the best environment in which to raise a child.

The Battle to Be a Parent[1]

By Richard Tate
The Advocate, January 30, 2001

When 10-year-old Miguel Washington was born, his mother, a mentally disabled woman living in an assisted-care facility, was unable to care for him. His father's whereabouts were unknown. When he was just 8 days old, Miguel was sent to live with his uncle, Paul Washington Jr., a single gay man.

"When my father [Paul Washington Sr.] called and told me my sister had given birth to Miguel," recalls Washington Jr., "I immediately offered to take him in. The fact that I'm gay has always been a bit of an issue with my family, but at the time and in this situation, it didn't seem to be a problem."

For almost 10 years, Washington Jr. raised his nephew in Cathedral City, Calif., without any problems. Helping him was Timothy Forrester, a special-education teacher whom Washington Jr. met and fell in love with when Miguel was 18 months old.

Then on October 6, 2000, Miguel left for an overnight fishing trip with his grandfather and didn't come home. The following day Washington Jr. and Forrester received a letter from a Los Angeles law firm representing the elder Washington. The letter informed the couple that Miguel had been removed from their custody and cited Miguel's participation in ballet and a "gay art class" as evidence that the two men were "actively promoting or influencing a gay lifestyle for the minor." Though Washington Jr. and Forrester had cared for Miguel all his life, suddenly their ability to parent was being called into question because of prejudice within their own family.

Though the circumstances of Miguel's case are exceptional, custody battles and fights over visitation rights have become increasingly common for gay and lesbian families in the wake of the late-'90s gay baby boom. "We've been involved with hundreds of these cases in the past year," says Patricia Logue, senior counsel for Lambda Legal Defense and Education Fund, a gay legal group. "And for every case we actually attach our name to, there are a hundred others we're assisting in some way."

The cases are the latest legal frontier for gays and lesbians. Twenty years ago, says Kate Kendell, executive director of the National Center for Lesbian Rights, gay parents were typically involved in custody hearings or visitation disputes only after coming out of heterosexual relationships.

---

1. Article by Richard Tate from *The Advocate* January 30, 2001. Copyright © *The Adcocate*. Reprinted with permission.

"At that time gay men and lesbians were routinely denied custody of the children they helped raise," Kendell explains. "However, in the last 10 years there has been a significant decrease in these kinds of cases. Not only have the parents who've fought these custody battles helped effect change, but also the sheer number of children affected and growing level of public awareness have all combined to assure that, in most cases, sexual orientation is not an issue."

According to Lambda, there are as many as 10 million gay and lesbian parents in the United States, mothers and fathers to as many as 14 million children. But because gay parents are not always biological parents, their rights are not universally protected, and laws and legal precedents regarding custody issues vary widely from state to state.

"Sexual orientation in and of itself is less a factor in some courts and still a major factor in others," says Logue. "In some parts of the country, courts are still questioning whether gay men and lesbians are fit to raise children or whether they should be allowed visitation rights. But when the focus is on the actual family—the actual nurturing and parenting—we're able to put the reality before the myth and are often successful in securing our rights."

That is the challenge the younger Washington is currently facing. He has had to establish that he is indeed Miguel's parent, because the bond was never legally established. Soon after he began caring for his nephew Washington Jr., now 50, contacted Los Angeles County Child Protective Services to inquire about securing legal custody of Miguel. He received a letter from the agency indicating that the proposed arrangements for Miguel, agreed on by his family, seemed to be in order and that a custody hearing would be set up. But, Washington Jr. says, the agency never followed through.

He had cause to reconsider the issue a few years later. "About five years ago, my father and his wife sat me down and expressed concerns," he says. "But their concerns were purely based in homophobia. They said Miguel needed to be raised around women, that [Tim and I] should not be physically demonstrative in front of him—that we needed to 'give Miguel's heterosexuality a chance.'" The conversation prompted him and Forrester to further investigate how they might establish legal custody of Miguel, perhaps even adopt him. "But it was so expensive," recalls Washington Jr. The attorney we spoke with mentioned that we might lose Miguel in the process, which terrified us. Things seemed OK as they were—people called us the 'gay poster family of the desert—and the legal costs would have altered our lifestyle in a way that would have been detrimental to Miguel, so we decided not to pursue it."

But when Miguel was removed from the couple's care by his grandfather last October, Washington Jr. and Forrester realized how tenuous their rights to custody really were. Authorities were unable to determine who had legal custody of the boy, although he had lived with his uncle and his uncle's partner virtually all of his life. Washington Jr. and Forrester were forced to go to court to obtain temporary custody of the child they'd raised as their own. In a landmark decision on October 9, the court granted joint temporary custody of Miguel to Washington Jr. and Forrester, legitimizing their family unit. Washington Sr., however, immediately sought to have the ruling overturned. When a judge denied the motion, Miguel's grandfather defied the court order that Miguel be returned to Washington Jr. and Forrester and instead sent his grandson to live with straight relatives in Pennsylvania.

Though Miguel was eventually returned to his uncle and Forrester, the legal battle over who should have custody of Miguel was just beginning. In an effort to settle the dispute between Miguel's fathers and grandparents, a judge postponed a December 8 custody hearing in favor of court-mandated counseling for the parties involved. At that appearance, Washington Jr. and Forrester were referred to in open court as Miguel's "two dads," and the denial of a motion to remove Forrester as a de facto parent seems a positive

---

"The legal fact is that most states no longer see a parent's sexual orientation alone as a basis for limiting parental rights."—Kate Kendell, the National Center for Lesbian Rights.

---

sign that the court may ultimately grant the couple joint custody. But as tension increases, even a full custody hearing, now scheduled for March 2, may not bring an end to the dispute.

In California there is no precedent for removing a child from the care of a parent or legal guardian solely based on his or her sexual orientation, and Washington Jr. says his attorneys are confident that he and Forrester will not lose Miguel. However, even if they are granted permanent custody of Miguel, the ruling could be appealed. Like many gays and lesbians raising children, Washington Jr. and Forrester are being forced to fight for their rights as parents amid suggestions that their sexual identity makes them unfit for the role.

Like their heterosexual counterparts, nonbiological gay parents often are able to win visitation rights to see the children they've helped raise by riding on the coattails of the established rights of nonadoptive parents, most commonly legal stepparents. Still, when the end of a relationship is contentious, the sexual orientation of the parents can become an issue in the legal wrangling that follows.

We've seen a precipitous increase in visitation and custody disputes between gay and lesbian couples," says Kendell. She says the cases, ugly as they may be, have had a positive effect on the law. "The legal fact is that most states no longer see a parent's sexual orientation alone as a basis for limiting parental rights."

Even for gay and lesbian parents in stable relationships, legally protecting their children can be difficult. Second-parent adoption, in which one partner seeks to adopt the other partner's children, is a crucial issue for same-sex couples raising children together. It's the only real way to provide custody rights to a surviving parent in the event of one partner's death, to protect a child's right to inheritance, and to ensure that children qualify for health care insurance and other benefits under both parents. But because many states require that the biological parents waive their right to custody before an individual other than a legal spouse is allowed to adopt a child, second-parent adoption is often problematic for gay parents. The cost and the intense scrutiny placed on parents in the process is daunting.

"I did it myself, for my 4-year-old son," says Kendell. "Now nothing can diminish the fact that I'm legally recognized as his parent. But the truth is that it was a very expensive process—upward of $3,000—and social workers came to my home to observe my family. I was required to answer very personal questions. It was invasive." Still, Kendell says, gay couples who can take advantage of second-parent adoption should do so.

State legislatures last year presented nonbiological gay and lesbian parents with one significant victory and one major setback with regard to adoption rights. In May the Connecticut general assembly overwhelmingly supported a bill allowing second-parent adoption, and in June, Gov. John G. Rowland signed the bill into law, making Connecticut the first state to protect the practice though legislation. However, this victory came on the heels of a disappointing move by lawmakers in Mississippi, who passed a law barring gay men and lesbians from adopting. A similar law was taken off the books in New Hampshire in 1999, but Mississippi is now the fourth state—along with Arkansas, Florida, and Utah—to limit the rights of gay and lesbian parents.

However, state courts rather than state legislatures most often dictate the outcome of custody battles, and in 2000 courts made significant steps toward recognizing the rights of gay parents. In April a New Jersey court granted visitation rights to a lesbian who helped raise her former partner's twins for the first two years of their lives. The court referred to the biological mother's ex as the twins' "psychological mother" and determined that she was, therefore, entitled to visitation rights. In what could be considered a de facto victory for nonbiological gay and lesbian parents, in October the U.S. Supreme Court declined to hear an appeal of the ruling, allowing the lower court's decision to stand.

Lending further credibility to the idea of psychological parenting, in October a judge in New York granted a woman permanent visitation rights to see the two children she helped raise, in spite of the objection of her former partner, the biological mother. Persuaded by the testimony of a child psychologist, the court determined that it was in the best interests of the children involved "to see both parents." Lawyers in the case called the ruling the first of its kind in the state.

Kendell says 2000 was a pivotal year in terms of the legal recognition of gay and lesbian families. "It's fair to say that we may have turned a corner with these cases, with courts now looking at the factual reality of family life and focusing less on the strict legal constructs of the statutes involved," she says. "In fact, it was the first year in which we actually won more cases than we lost."

In May a Maryland appeals court ruled that an ex-partner in a lesbian relationship could have legal standing similar to that of a stepparent, though the court stopped short of equating the legal status of same-sex partnership with that of heterosexual ones. While visitation rights were not granted because of the emotional problems of the child involved, the ruling affirmed the rights of nonbiological gay parents.

Also in May another ruling in favor of gay parents came out of Florida. There, the district court of appeals reversed the 1998 ruling of a trial court that had granted sole custody of two young children to their father, removing them from the care of their lesbian mother and her partner. The court condemned the antigay sentiment in such custody battles by stating that the lower court inappropriately "succumbed to the father's attacks on the mother's sexual orientation."

However, not all of the high-profile custody cases of 2000 had positive outcomes. Gay parents in Pennsylvania saw the courts limit their rights to adopt when in November the state superior court denied second-parent adoption rights to two couples—one lesbian, one gay—in spite of the fact that such adoptions have been done frequently in many Pennsylvania counties. The court's ruling clearly stated that same-sex partners do not have the same legal standing as heterosexual couples in second-parent adoption cases. The case, a major setback for gay and lesbian parents, came down to a strict interpretation of state law. The court cited the state adoption act, which extends second-parent adoption rights to spouses of biological parents. But because gay marriage is not legal in the state, the court said, partners of gay men and lesbians are not legally considered spouses and therefore have no right to adopt the biological children of their partners.

"It's obvious to me that legal marriage represents the Holy Grail in terms of legal protections for our families," says Kendell, who admits to reservations about the institution of marriage. "But as a lawyer, the conclusion is inescapable: Not having legal marriage will always relegate our families and relationships to second-class status."

Still, there is hope. In what might be considered a small victory, superior court judge Correale Stevens, author of the majority in the Pennsylvania case, made it clear that the court's ruling was dictated by the letter of the law, not the sexual orientation of the couples seeking adoption rights. It is the job of the legislature, not the judiciary, the court said, to expand existing laws to recognize same-sex partners.

The dissenting opinion, however, said the court inappropriately focused on the same-sex relationship between the parents rather than the relationships between parents and child, suggesting that the interests of the children were being ignored. The Pennsylvania case is one example of many heard in courtrooms across the country every year. And as the courts and legislatures continue to determine the boundaries of gay parents' rights, what is becoming clear is that the rights of the children of gay parents, the most important but often forgotten participants in custody disputes, are being established as well.

"Overall, 2000 was positive year," says Logue. "Much has been added to the foundation. Though custody disputes can be disheartening, our families are being recognized and validated more than ever."

Confessions of a Black Mr. Mom[2]

By Ta-Nehisi Coates
The Washington Monthly, March 2002

In one of his more interesting comic sketches, Chris Rock compares one group of African Americans, "niggas," to another more wholesome group, "black people." "You know what really bugs me about niggas is the way they always take credit for stuff a normal man would just do," says Rock. "Like, 'I raised my kids.'"

By Rock's definition, I know exactly where I belong among African-Americans today. For I am sure that even for this meager deed of fatherhood I am performing, I deserve a lot more than credit. My mission sounds simple enough: carting my young son through West Manhattan to visit another friend, working in Chelsea. I have logged enough baby hours to earn the title "stay-at-home dad," so I'm not exactly new to this. But our trek into the city elicits terror because of three converging factors: 1) I am a hefty 6'4" black male—anything can happen. 2) It's Manhattan—everything might happen. 3) My son is 7 months old—something always happens.

To take the mystery out of the island on this visit to New York, I have recruited two friends. It helps that they are native New Yorkers and know the geography. It doesn't help that they are also young, black, male writers, whose size and dress (like my own), says almost nothing about who they are. Pushing the stroller, I remember the last time I was in New York with two other black male writers. As we were emerging from a Brooklyn subway that day, a white lady coming down the steps glanced our way and when she did not see Langston Hughes, immediately reversed direction.

Complicating things further today, the clouds that have been threatening us all afternoon open up with all their lordly might. Thunder and showers are everywhere. I suggest a cab. My friends remind me that we are the bane of taxis the realm over. But at least with a stroller we have a chance at netting a compassionate driver, right? Several yellow drive-bys later, we trot off with this one truth: Not even a stroller and a wet infant can take the monster out of three black dudes on a corner.

We walk the next several blocks in the rain to reach our goal. Our taxi episode initiates a contest for who has the worst "cabbies hate black men" story. I think I could win, were I focused on sorting

2. Reprinted with permission from *The Washington Monthly.* Copyright by Washington Monthly Publishing, LLC, 733 15th St. NW, Suite 1000, Washington, DC 20005. (202) 393-5155. Web site: *www.washingtonmonthly.com.*

through my "Astonishing Tales of Negrophobia" database. But I am too busy dealing with my own phobia—the one of my partner.

Samori Maceo-Paul Coates is the big-headed result of my union with Kenyatta Matthews. We met during a mutual stint at Howard University and have been together ever since. Before we met, she had a dim view of men as fathers. Her plan for parenthood was basically: get pregnant by some dude and then conveniently lose him. A father would only complicate things, she thought. When she got pregnant with Samori, I was able to convince her otherwise, but during my time as a dad, I have given my share of evidence to bolster her original view, and today's trip in the rain only promises to add another letter to the file.

> *The idealistic black father is left to wonder, "Did Gandhi have to contend with crappy diapers?"*

Until now, Samori has been the picture of health. I am not even sure I've heard him cough. If he comes down with anything from this jaunt through the elements, Kenyatta will make worm's food of me. As if I needed confirmation of this, when we arrive in Chelsea, our host squeezes Samori's drenched pullover, then looks at me and keenly notes, "You're dead."

Thankfully, I make it back into Brooklyn before Kenyatta gets home from work. By the time she walks in, Samori is sound asleep, with no cough to speak of. Only his damp clothes, hanging on a door like discarded snakeskin, give a clue to our ordeal. But either out of fatigue or forbearance—it matters not which—she decides to save the haranguing for another day. And there will be another day. Indeed, for the black dude attempting to be June Cleaver—a man standing at the nexus of two undervalued experiences—this is his lot. Everywhere he looks there is another burden, be it the glare of his partner, or the blind eye of a cabbie. But in his own mind at least, he is a hero.

You see, for black men like me, fatherhood is a mission, a chance to atone for all the legions of errant black fathers. The black stay-at-home dad in particular gains purpose from all of this, and convinces himself of his own Gandhi-like nobility. Of course, most of this mental crusading occurs before the kid pops into the world, and the idealistic black father is left to wonder, "Did Gandhi have to contend with crappy diapers?"

Deadbeats by the Dozen

If you believe the people who study such things, the odds of my becoming a responsible father were slim to none. On paper, according to both liberal and conservative models, my demographic profile should make me a deadbeat. I'm a young, black, underemployed male who fathered a child out of wedlock. I also grew up in the center of the absent-dad epidemic, in which it was so common for black men to abandon their children that there was no longer much shame in it.

In high school in Baltimore, it seemed that I didn't have a single class where there wasn't a young lady who either had a child, was pregnant, or both. The fathers were much harder to identify, and more anonymous, I suspect, because many of them were older. Even at plush, thor-

> *Deadbeat dads rank about one step below the Klan in popularity among African Americans.*

oughly middle-class Howard University, many of my fellow students were absent parents. In my last year in school, I remember meeting a dude from some small town in Pennsylvania. I was shocked when he told me he had a child. He was unemployed and pursuing an undergrad degree, and really had no means of supporting a child.

"Where's the baby and the mother?" I asked

"Back home," he said, smiling at a joke that I didn't find funny.

When Kenyatta first became pregnant, I never thought twice about embracing fatherhood. Even as we weighed our options, all I could think about was this grand opportunity to join the ranks of present and accountable fathers. My fervor sprang from all the typical reasons people give for having children—mainly a desire to see a continuance of my gene pool. But there were other reasons, fraught with sociological implications.

For as long as I can remember, I have wanted to be a father, if only because I knew so few. You don't need to grow up in the projects or abysmal poverty to know that black fathers are in short supply. If you assembled all the dads in my working-class Baltimore neighborhood, you might have the starting five for a basketball team. Of course, they would lose to the moms, who would have a bench, a coaching staff, a mascot, and the home-court advantage. With such a depressing backdrop, those African-American fathers who elect to be more than a sperm bank become de facto heroes, demi-gods born out of utter desperation.

Much conservative ink has been spilled boiling the problems of black America down to its absent daddies, but no one in the black community needs pundits to lecture him on family values. Deadbeat dads rank about one step below the Klan in popularity among African Americans. Hiphop may be grossly misogynistic, but you will be hard pressed to find a cultural movement that more reveres mothers and reviles fathers. (Indeed, rap's only mother-hater of note is a white guy, Eminem.) The anti-paternal sentiment in rap expresses a larger fatigue among African Americans for "tired-ass" black men who doom kids to fatherless lives. So when Jay-Z says "Momma loves me, Pop I miss you/God help me forgive 'em, I got some issues," he isn't simply having a cathartic moment, he is speaking for 70 percent of African-American children. He is also speaking for my partner and me.

My own father's pedigree—seven kids by four women—looks like the rap sheet for one more deadbeat. But he was a stable and consistent presence in my home. And yet so dismal is his context that my siblings and I often find ourselves in the absurd situation of listing among his virtues the fact that he actually acknowledged all of us.

But after the solid presence of my father, the search for men of substance in Samori's lineage disintegrates into a trail of figures who could claim the title "father" only in the coldest sense of the word. My paternal grandfather sired so many kids that no one has an accurate count of his seeds. My father last saw him alive when he was nine. My mother's father abandoned his wife and five kids when my mother was a child. When I was a kid she boldly tracked him down with me in tow, only to be told that we both must now call him "Raymond."

Kenyatta, like my mother, is the product of a daddy on the lam. And her maternal grandfather, theoretically present in her mother's life, was a spousal abuser and a suspected child molester who died in bed with another woman. The result of all these paternal shenanigans is a patchwork family tree, with Kenyatta's father and grandfather's family completely blotted out.

From this perverse montage of ghost dads, I gleaned a somewhat melodramatic message: To be a father is the most noble calling an African-American man can ever undertake. Viewed within the historical context of racism and lynching, to me, the black father was a soldier taking up the sword and banner of a disgraced order of knights.

I was not alone in this belief. To whip up popular appeal for the 1994 Million Man March, Louis Farrakhan declared war on no-account black men, and singled out deadbeat dads in particular. It was a brilliant tactic and struck a chord in the black community as nothing had since the Civil Rights movement. I was at the Million Man March, but I didn't need Farrakhan to declare war on deadbeat dads for me. I would do it myself, by taking a shot at fathering a child as soon as I felt I had the means to raise one. That moment came a little sooner than I'd expected, but when Kenyatta got pregnant, and we began hashing out the possibilities, I really only had one in mind. I would join a citizen army, restore honor to the tattered banner of black fatherhood, and hoist it high for all to see.

What to Expect When You're Expecting

As Kenyatta and I evaluated our situation, it soon became clear that it made fiscal sense for Samori to stay at home with me for his first year. My career as a freelance writer could continue from home, while Kenyatta could continue her copyediting work in the field.

For some men, becoming Mr. Mom may have seemed a severe form of emasculation. But my own father had been a stay-at-home dad—for many years my mother was the breadwinner in the family—and he was manly enough to be a Black Panther when that meant something. So when my turn came, I moved pretty easily into my role as keeper of the hearth. In preparation, I began to bone up on my cooking skills, already a hobby of mine, and pored over *What to Expect When You're Expecting*.

For the first two weeks after Samori was born, we had Kenyatta's mother to lean on. When she returned to Chicago, Kenyatta was still available to handle swing-shift feedings, so my real tenure as a stay-at-home dad didn't begin until Samori was three months old, when Kenyatta returned to work. Even then, contending with all those diapers on my own, I was still caught up in the romance of being a black daddy, and one who, at least in his own mind, was very good at it.

Indeed, accolades rolled my way at first. Women who witnessed even the simplest display of my baby-handling techniques were wont to melt into a chorus of "awwws." My multifaceted identity allowed me to cross borders; I could easily move from a conversation weighing breast milk against formula to another weighing Barry Sanders against Emmitt Smith.

The black Mr. Mom is still black before he is a Mr. Mom. And quite frankly, he is still a Mr. before he is a Mom.

But of course, some borders are never crossed: The black Mr. Mom is still black before he is a Mr. Mom. And quite frankly, he is still a Mr. before he is a Mom. Reality quickly came crashing into my one-man dad's group. I could deal with the relatively few old ladies who used to think twice about crossing my path. But now it was those same old ladies, emboldened by the presence of a stroller, who wanted to launch an inquisition into my parenting skills. I found myself regularly interrogated by panic-stricken strangers: Is that a rash? Should you be carrying that boy on your shoulders like that? Is that jacket thick enough? I became especially nervous when visiting my parents. If Samori looked as if he were about to cry, my mom would interrupt whatever measures I was taking, swoop in, and proceed with her own time-tested methods.

On top of all that, before Samori was even born, I unwittingly made my tour of duty especially rigorous. I was a 24-year-old college dropout and freelance journalist. By that description, you can probably get a ballpark figure of my income. Despite heavy family pressure, my partner and I are not married (hence the term partner) and have pretty much ruled it out for the time being. When she got pregnant I moved into her apartment, which she didn't mind paying for by herself.

In more than a few sectors of America, there are highly technical terms for unemployed college dropouts who are supported by their pregnant girlfriends—bum and freeloader the most common ones.

But in the black community, where there is an involuntary tradition of working moms and unemployed dads, the nomenclature is even more defined: no-good-nigga being the current label of choice.

Snide comments about our living situation filtered in from all quarters. At a family cookout, a woman cornered Kenyatta and lectured her on the need to "trap" me into marriage. Once, while interviewing a source for a story, I made the mistake of mentioning I was a dad living in sin. A 10-minute lecture on God's intentions for family pretty much killed the story.

Yet through it all, I was never sorry for the choice I had made. And eventually, I found my community more supportive than I had imagined. My mother's meddlings with Samori sometimes annoyed me, but when I needed to go back to work full-time, she also ponied up $400 every month for day care. I hated the interrogations from women on the street. And yet, it's very hard to equal the high of pushing a stroller up Brooklyn's Flatbush Avenue and seeing a black woman about your mother's age shoot you a smile that says, "You done right, boy."

It's very hard to equal the high of pushing a stroller . . . and seeing a black woman about your mother's age shoot you a smile that says, "You done right, boy."

Boys to Men

How did I end up doing right when so many of my peers have done wrong? I had some help at home. My mother was an uncompromising advocate of responsible fatherhood. Her non-relationship with her father hung overhead constantly, as well as the specter of what she called "nothing men."

Whenever my path appeared to stray, particularly as a teen, I think my mom must have seen visions of raising a man like her father. In these instances, her eyes would flash and even though I was several inches taller than her by then, she would still snatch me up, wrench my arm with one hand and jab my chest with the index finger of another. Boring through my eyes with hers, she would swear that she was raising a lot of things under her roof, but she wasn't raising "niggas to hang on the corner."

Even in moments when I had committed no transgression, I was treated to lectures on my responsibility to self, family, and the black community. Always frank with me about taboo subjects like teen pregnancy, my mom had a rule: If a girl showed up to my house and claimed she was carrying my child, paternity tests were not an option. If I'd had sex with her, I was the father, and my mother expected me to take responsibility for that child. And yet, I don't think that even my mom's diatribes against deadbeat dads were much different than any other black mother's. What made a difference for me, I think, was the example of my father.

On the surface, my father could not be mistaken for Cliff Huxtable. He was the product of abject poverty in Philadelphia, a high-school dropout. Before meeting my mother, he had already fathered five kids by three different women. But while her family was horrified by his gaggle of illegitimate children, my mom was attracted by the fact that he always seemed to be toting one or two of those kids around.

In theory, I suppose, my father probably qualified as a deadbeat in the sense that he provided little financial support for his large family. He never had any money. But what he lacked in money, he made up for with time. By the time I was born, my father had left the Black Panthers. But he still carried on his political activities, and tried to drill them into his kids. He dragged us around to black-nationalist events and he made us read little books on famous black people such as W. E. B. Du Bois. Thanks to him, I even was forced to endure a bout of "self-esteem work" in one of those Afrocentric rites-of-passage programs.

My dad also served as the "no-shit dude," who, as we got older, ran something of a reform school for kids—his kids—when they were teetering on the edge of serious trouble. When the mothers of his other children reached the point of exasperation with their teenage sons, those sons were often sent to live with us (I lived with both my mother and father). My father served as disciplinarian, and somehow managed to help my mother steer all of us back from the brink. He wasn't all bark, though. My fondest memories are of my father—a cooking enthusiast—gathering all his kids at his house and preparing a Maryland feast of crab cakes, fried whiting, hush puppies, and shrimp.

Oddly enough, the family feast idea was something he'd picked up from his own father, who was no Ward Cleaver. Aside from his many unclaimed children, my grandfather was also, by all accounts, a woman-beater and vicious disciplinarian. And yet if you ask my father what he remembers of him, he will tell you he remembers his father gathering all his kids together whenever possible, for whatever quality time he could.

My father's attempts to replicate those gatherings—and then some—show how far a good example can go towards creating a decent parent. Indeed, the combination of my father's example served us better than any rites-of-passage program could have. There are seven of us kids now. All except one of the four boys have children of our own. Some of us are married, most aren't. But there are no deadbeats among us.

Multiplying Mr. Moms

Many middle-class people, especially white ones, will think that my father should never have had all those kids in the first place. Likewise, to mainstream America, I am not exactly a hero for staying home to take care of my son, but irresponsible for having sired the child in the first place without finishing college, getting a good job, and securing a wedding ring. Yet if more men whose children weren't born under the most perfect of circumstances did what I did, the nation's black children would be far better off than they are now.

Farrakhan was right in calling on men to return to the family, but his insistence that they assume the traditional role of provider, while women submit to them, was highly misguided. After all, no black woman was going to take that submissive stuff seriously, and given the realities of the economy, a lot of dads, especially young ones, aren't going to become venture capitalists before their kids reach draft age.

Perhaps, instead of focusing so much on the check-writing aspect of fatherhood or trying to marry off unwilling partners for the children's sake, it's time for a political movement that seeks to transform "no-good niggas" into an army of Mr. Moms. Since no one has figured out how to make black men much richer, or married, for that matter, why not at least take advantage of the one asset we have in abundance: our time. For instance, instead of throwing young guys in jail when they fail to pay child support they couldn't possibly pay, how about making them babysit (with a few parenting classes first) while their children's mothers go to work?

Not only would the children be better off, but their fathers might actually discover what I already know: that fatherhood is fun, and that it really is the noble calling that I had envisioned, despite the crappy diapers.

Love Without Borders[3]

By Lynette Clemetson
Newsweek, September 18, 2000

Ah, weddings. The hair, the makeup, the layers of fabric. They're enough to frazzle the calmest of brides. But when Taiwanese-American Grace Tsai married Japanese-Canadian Richard Tsuyuki, she took wedding-day stress to a whole new level. After a Roman Catholic ceremony in a New Jersey church, the wedding party dashed to a banquet hall in Philadelphia's Chinatown. There was the waltz, the cake and the bouquet toss. Then the new Mrs. Tsuyuki rushed to a back room, took off her white gown and returned in a slim-fitting, high-necked Chinese *chipao* dress for a customary tea ceremony. As guests dug into a 14-course Chinese meal, she dashed out, changed into an elaborate Japanese kimono and reappeared for a sake-drinking ritual. By the time the bride raised her tiny cup of Japanese wine, she was ready for a drink. "It was totally crazy and exhausting," she says. "But it was important for us to melt together our different cultures."

Americans are melting together like never before. A 1998 Census survey tallied more than 1.3 million racially mixed marriages in the United States. And that didn't include interethnic couples like Grace and Richard. As the nonwhite population becomes more diverse, the number of interethnic marriages is fast increasing. Roughly one in six Asian-Americans is married to an Asian of a different ethnic background. Latinos are intermarrying in similar numbers. "Because we're a society obsessed with race, interethnic marriages fall under a cloak of invisibility," says demographer Larry Shinagawa. "But in fact, these unions are reshaping our concept of ethnicity."

Invisibility has its rewards. When Grace and Richard stroll down the suburban streets near their home in Sterling, Va., they are spared the obvious stares that white and black mixed couples sometimes face. To the majority of Americans, the features that would mark them as ethnically different in Asia (the shape of their eyes and curve of their faces) go completely unnoticed. But the assumption of cultural affinity can also be annoying. "People look at us and they see us as generically Asian," says Richard, "when in reality we have to deal with cultural clashes like other mixed couples."

---

3. From *Newsweek*, September 18, 2000 © 2000 Newsweek, Inc. All rights reserved.

Their differences are never more pronounced than when dealing with family. Though Grace grew up in Bordentown, N.J., her home life was traditional Taiwanese, filled with live-in extended family and lots of raucous chatter. To Richard, who was raised in a strict, Japanese family in Winnipeg, Canada, where his father was the sole voice of authority, the onslaught of Grace's lively relatives often feels like chaos. His sometimes standoffish demeanor can unwittingly cause offense. For Grace, the subtle Japanese nuances of nondirectness are as frustrating as a foreign language. "The phrase 'I want' is not part of their traditional style," she says.

> ## "After the third generation they are all Americanized."—Song Tsai, Taiwanese father.

But for couples like the Tsuyukis, bridging the cross-cultural waters is about more than preserving family harmony. On some level it is also about rejecting Old World baggage and grasping for a shared American identity. A generation ago, their marriage would have been scandalous to relatives with bad memories of war and occupation. And even today there are a few left in the family tree who rationalize the union with the notion that it could have been worse. "At least he's not mainland Chinese," some of Grace's Taiwanese clan might mumble. "At least she's Asian and not white," some of Richard's Japanese relatives may reason. To Grace and Richard the old-school divisiveness just doesn't make sense. "'United we stand' is so much smarter for us as a people," says Grace. "Even if living it is not always that easy."

The trick is to build on shared values without losing treasured customs and traditions. It is a challenge Grace and Richard will soon face. They are expecting their first child, a girl, in October. They plan to choose a Japanese first name that can be shortened to an English-sounding nickname, and a Chinese middle name, chosen based on the date and time of the birth. They are amassing a library filled with Japanese children's songs, Chinese folk tales and Dr. Seuss. The nursery will have ABCs along one wall, Chinese characters on another and modern Japanese characters on a third. "We're committed to preserving the richness of our cultures," says Richard.

The grandparents-to-be are resigned to what they see as an inevitable cultural dilution. "Let's face it. After the third generation they are all Americanized," says Grace's father, Song Tsai, 61. "It's natural. This baby will be part of the melting pot." Grace and Richard believe they have held onto more of their heritage than either of their families realize. Still, how their traditions change in the next generation will have much to do with how American diversity develops. "What if our daughter grows up and marries a Filipino-Korean?" muses Richard. "What will her child be?" Grace looks puzzled for a moment, then responds. "Maybe she'll just be Asian," she says. "Or maybe she'll just be . . . American."

The trick is to build on shared heritage without losing cherished traditions.

The End of the Family?[4]

By Terry Golway
America, July 16–23, 2001

You've heard the news, no doubt. The American family is changing. No, not just changing—it is being revolutionized. New models
are replacing the old. The traditional family, announced one of the
great newsweeklies, is fading fast. Who needs a husband? asks
another. On the op-ed page of the *New York Times*, the columnist
Frank Rich delights in reminding all who will listen that the days of
the Cleaver family are long gone, a cultural event Rich finds
immensely satisfying.

Yes, you've been hearing about this for some time, and when the
Census Bureau released its snapshot of life in the United States in
the year 2000, you heard a lot more. The census numbers were trot-
ted out to ratify the impressionistic, anecdotal conclusions reached
years ago: yes, the traditional family is fading fast, America.

Or is it?

The media, particularly slick magazines and the cable-television
shockathons, bombarded us right around Mother's Day with stories
built around census data showing that more kids than ever live in
single-parent households. And that trend, they reported—no, they
celebrated—will continue in the coming decades.

There is certainly no denying that more kids today live with one
parent than in the 1950s, that decade that seems to stir so much
anger in so many people for reasons that rarely seem coherent. But
there is quite another way to look at the data used to celebrate the
end of the traditional family. After decades of divorce and family
breakdown, 75 percent of white children live with two parents—
that's three out of four, down from nine out of 10, but a surprisingly
high figure given all the hype in recent years. Among black children,
36 percent live with two parents, compared to 58 percent in 1970.
But wait. There's an uptick in the percentage of black children in
two-parent households. The single-parent trend actually topped out
in the mid-1990s, and has begun to decrease. Among Hispanic children, the same is true—64 percent live in two-parent households,
down from 78 percent in 1970 but up slightly since the mid-1990s.

So what about the end of the traditional American family? Could it
be that folks in the media are exaggerating just a little bit? One of
the newsweeklies offered an approving sidebar of a young woman
who has had three children by three different men and has married
none of them. Her kids have asked her why she doesn't get married.

She replied—and her reply was written in large, headline type—"I had the kids. Why should I marry?" (Well, ma'am, rather than talk about you, let's talk about what's best for your children. . . .)

The media's reporting of the changing American family—and make no mistake, it is changing, and sometimes for the better—is filled with the bias of false inclusion, so much so that any parent who lives with a spouse and children could hardly be blamed for thinking that he or she is a cultural anachronism. And anybody who insists, as most level-headed people would, that two parents are better than one is immediately dismissed as a right-wing fanatic, a borderline cultural fascist, who seeks to impose outdated ideas of morality and family on others.

It surely is true that many single parents are heroic; it is also fair to say that many heroic single parents would rather not be single at all. Most are moms whose partners or husbands are out of the picture, for whatever reason.

And certainly it is heartwarming to see single men or women willing to adopt children—infants who might have been aborted, or baby girls faced with grim futures in cultures where boys still are preferred. Sadly, too, many parents, mostly women, probably are better off alone than with abusive spouses.

Two-parent families are hopelessly archaic and—worst of all!—ridiculously unhip? Certainly not.

Yes, society is far more tolerant of single parents than it used to be. Is that the same as saying that the traditional family is dying, or that two-parent families are hopelessly archaic and—worst of all!—ridiculously unhip? Certainly not.

Certainly the church, at the pastoral level, has become far more understanding of the complex problems in which families find themselves.

Parishes reach out to single parents, divorced and otherwise. Most of us know a one-parent family, and appreciate that whatever happened between two adults, the children and the parents are deserving of love and support.

All the same, there is something disturbing about the media's enthusiasm for nontraditional families, and the speed with which they have declared the traditional family dead—even, or especially, when the data actually indicate otherwise. It may be nothing more than a misguided attempt to make everybody feel nice and warm and fuzzy. Maybe it's just a gimmick to get other people to write indignant columns denouncing a magazine cover or a network television report. Or, given the rather complicated personal lives of some of our media elites, maybe it's just projection.

Perhaps this dutiful correspondent lives in a cultural bubble, but every Sunday—no, every day—I see lots of two-parent families in my little town in New Jersey, and they not only seem happy, but utterly and completely vital.

They are stories waiting to be discovered. And maybe, when the media are again looking for some photogenic trend, they will be.

Bibliography

Books

Cain, Madelyn. *The Childless Revolution: What It Means to Be Childless Today*. Cambridge, Mass: Perseus Publishing, 2002.

Casper, Lynne M., and Suzanne M. Bianchi. *Continuity & Change in the American Family*. Thousand Oaks, Calif: Sage Publications, 2002.

Coontz, Stephanie. *The Way We Really Are: Coming to Terms with America's Changing Families*. New York: BasicBooks, 1997.

Hertz, Frederick. *Legal Affairs: Essential Advice for Same-Sex Couples*. New York: H. Holt and Co., 1998.

Hochschild, Arlie Russell. *The Time Bind: When Work Becomes Home and Home Becomes Work*. New York : Metropolitan Books, 1997.

Jeffers, Susan. *I'm Okay . . . You're a Brat: Setting the Priorities Straight and Freeing You from the Guilt and Mad Myths of Parenthood*. Los Angeles: Renaissance Books, 2000.

Kennedy, Randall. *Interracial Intimacies: Sex, Marriage, Identity, and Adoption*. New York: Pantheon, 2002.

Kindlon, Dan. *Too Much of a Good Thing: Raising Children of Character in an Indulgent Age*. New York: Hyperion, 2001.

Lehr, Valerie. *Queer Family Values: Debunking the Myth of the Nuclear Family*. Philadelphia: Temple University Press, 1999.

Lerner, Harriet. *The Mother Dance: How Children Change Your Life*. New York: HarperCollins Publishers, 1998.

Newman, Margaret. *Stepfamily Realities: How to Overcome Difficulties and Have a Happy Family*. Oakland, Calif: New Harbinger Publications, 1994.

Papernow, Patricia L. *Becoming a Stepfamily: Patterns of Development in Remarried Families*. San Francisco: Jossey-Bass, 1993.

Waite, Linda J., and Maggie Gallagher. *The Case for Marriage: Why Married People Are Happier, Healthier, and Better Off Financially*. New York: Doubleday, 2000.

Wallenstein, Peter. *Tell the Court I Love My Wife: Race, Marriage, and Law*. New York: Palgrave Macmillan, 2002.

Wallerstein, Judith S., Julia M. Lewis, and Sandra Blakeslee. *The Unexpected Legacy of Divorce: A 25 Year Landmark Study*. New York: Hyperion, c2000.

Whitehead, Barbara Dafoe. *Why There Are No Good Men Left: The Romantic Plight of the New Single Woman*. New York: Broadway Books, 2003.

Wilson, James Q. *The Marriage Problem: How Our Culture Has Weakened Families*. New York: HarperCollins, c2002.

Zullo, Kathryn, and Allan Zullo. *The Nanas and the Papas: A Boomers' Guide to Grandparenting*. Kansas City: Andrews McMeel Pub., 1998.

Web Sites

Here is a list of Web sites for readers who would like more information on the American family or other related topics. Due to the Internet's ever-changing nature, the existence of a site is not guaranteed; however, at the time of this publication all Web sites were in existence and operational.

Alternatives to Marriage Project
www.unmarried.org

A nonprofit organization advocating equality for unmarried people, including those who choose not to marry, cannot marry, or live together before marriage.

American Association of Interchurch Families
http://www.aifw.org/aaif/index.htm

Serves as a support for families of two different Christian denominations. The group encourages couples to strengthen their relationship while maintaining an active role in two churches, and attempts to strengthen the Christian commitment of those whose attachment to their church has become nominal.

Child Abuse Prevention Network
http://child-abuse.com/

Provides support for child abuse prevention professionals and supplies lay readers with information about child abuse and the various child abuse programs in which they can become involved.

Childfree.net
www.childfree.net

For childless adults who wish to celebrate their freedom from the loss of personal liberty, money, time, and energy that having children requires.

Dovetail Institute for Interfaith Family Resources
www.dovetailinstitute.org

A nonprofit organization unaffiliated with any religious denomination, which strives to help Jewish and Christian partners explore the spiritual and religious dimensions of an interfaith household and conducts research of concern to interfaith families.

Freedom to Marry Project
www.freedomtomarry.org

Founded to advance the movement for marriage equality for gays and lesbians, with the goal of winning the freedom to marry in at least one state within the next five years.

Mothers & More
www.mothersandmore.org

A nonprofit organization for caregivers that provides mothers with opportunities to connect with one another and helps them to make transitions between family, work, and life.

National Adoption Information Clearinghouse
www.calib.com / naic

A national resource for professionals, policy makers, and the general public for information on all aspects of adoption.

National Campaign to Prevent Teen Pregnancy
www.teenpregnancy.org

An organization whose goal is to reduce the rate of teen pregnancy by one-third between 1996 and 2005.

National Coalition Against Domestic Violence
www.ncadv.org

Dedicated to the empowerment of battered women and their children through coalition-building at the local, state, regional, and national levels; support for the provision of safe homes and shelter programs for battered women and their children; public education; and policy development.

National Family Caregivers Association
www.nfcacares.org

Supports family caregivers and speaks out publicly for caregivers' needs.

National Fatherhood Initiative
www.fatherhood.org

A movement to improve the well-being of children by increasing the proportion of children growing up with involved, responsible, and committed fathers.

National Marriage Project at Rutgers University
marriage.rutgers.edu

Seeks to strengthen the institution of marriage by providing research and analysis to inform public policy and educate the American public about the problem with the growing rate of divorce.

Resolve (the National Infertility Association)
www.resolve.org

Dedicated to providing education, advocacy, and support to men and women struggling with infertility.

Stepfamily Foundation
www.stepfamily.org

Founded in 1976 to help solve problems that arise from the complex relationships in stepfamilies.

Additional Periodical Articles with Abstracts

More information on the American family and other related topics can be found in the following articles. Readers who are interested in additional articles may consult *Readers' Guide to Periodical Literature*, the *Social Sciences Index*, and other H.W. Wilson publications.

When Muslims and Christians Marry. Rita George Tvrtkovic. *America*, v. 185 pp11–14 September 10, 2001.

Tvrtkovic reports on a meeting held in February 2001 at the Cenacle Retreat House in Chicago to reflect on marriages between Christians and Muslims. Although most so-called mixed marriages involve Catholics and other Christians, increasing numbers of Catholics are marrying adherents of other religions. The pastoral needs of Christian-Muslim couples and the three major challenges they face are discussed.

The Marrying Kind. Jonathan Rauch. *Atlantic Monthly*, v. 289 p24 May 2002.

Rauch asserts that marriage is not being undermined by homosexuals who want to get married but by the fact that they can't get married. Cohabitation of couples has been on the rise for decades, whereas marriage is headed in the other direction. Cohabitation tends to be both less stable and less happy than marriage, but it is often viewed as a different-but-equal alternative. Conservatives are desperate to stave off same-sex marriage, many moderates remain queasy about legalizing gay marriage, and liberation-minded leftists were never very happy about matrimony to begin with. The vast majority of gays want the right to marry, but most agree that domestic-partner benefits are much better than nothing. Some conservatives insist that homosexuals would take their marital vows less seriously than heterosexuals, but this is doubtful. Marriage needs all the support and participation it can get, and homosexuals are pleading to move beyond cohabitation.

Women Work. The Support System Doesn't. Catherine Arnst. *Business Week,* p46 November 4, 2002.

The writer argues that while working mothers are the new hot topic in TV and books, Hollywood has failed to show that the support system for working mothers in America does not work. She points out that some women have been forced to drop out of the workforce due to the lack of affordable, high-quality child care; husbands willing to assume more of the child-rearing burden; and family-friendly work policies. She notes that this may be why such novels as *I Don't Know How She Does It: The Life of Kate Reddy, Working Mother*, by Allison Pearson, have struck such a chord.

Sex and the Marriage Market. James Q. Wilson. *Commentary*, v. 113 pp40–46 March 2002.

Wilson reports that the United States has suffered a dramatic rise in the number of single-parent, female-headed families. There are many explanations for this powerful change in U.S. society, but one explanation that is frequently overlooked is related to the number of men who are available to be married in the first place. America has had a low sex ratio—the number of men per hundred women in the society—in the last decades, and this shows no indication of changing significantly. The different effects the ratio has had on black and white Americans reveal that there is more to the issue than the sex ratio, however. The phenomenon is far from reducible to a single or simple cause, nor is it likely to be addressed by a single or simple policy.

Ending and Surviving an Abusive Relationship. Zondra Hughes. *Ebony*, v. 55 pp48–50 October 2000.

Hughes explains that African-American women often suffer domestic abuse in silence. The Department of Justice reports that every nine seconds a woman is threatened, bullied, beaten, or emotionally abused by her partner. Although many victims share similarities in the cycle of domestic abuse, black women often encounter huge racial and cultural odds that may impede their ability to seek professional help, according to experts. The writer provides ten strategies for ending the cycle of abuse.

Not All Women Cry the Baby Blues. Patricia Sellers. *Fortune*, v. 145 p30 May 13, 2002.

Claims that high-level businesswomen are suffering an epidemic of childlessness are not supported by a survey conducted at *Fortune's* Most Powerful Women in Business Summit. In *Creating a Life: Professional Women and the Quest for Children*, Sylvia Ann Hewlett says that 49 percent of women earning more than $100,000 are childless after age 40. In the *Fortune* survey, however, 71 percent have children and seem to have a better life-work balance than those surveyed by Hewlett. In addition, most of the high achievers consulted do not agree with Hewlett's theories.

What's Ahead for Families: Five Major Forces of Change. Joseph F. Coates. *The Futurist*, v. 30 pp27–33 September/October 1996.

Coates writes that important social trends are dramatically changing the future for families in America and elsewhere. Five trends and their implications for the family are discussed: structural changes in society, the rise of the two-income family, different patterns of divorce, the proliferation of the non-traditional family, and the increase in the number of seniors.

Is Divorce Too Easy? Benedict Carey. *Health*, v. 13 pp122–124 September 1999.

With growing evidence of the negative consequences of marital breakup, Carey reports that measures to make it harder to divorce are being advocated by an alliance of conservatives and feminists. In comparison to married persons, divorcees are far more likely to suffer depression, drink heavily, commit suicide, and develop heart disease and cancer. Moreover, women in particular suffer financially and emotionally as a result of divorce. America has the world's highest rate of divorce—between 40 and 50 percent of first-time marriages—and debate has been ongoing for decades as to how to lower this figure. In August 1997, Louisiana introduced an alternative option to the usual no-fault marriage contract that gives more power to a spouse who wishes to remain married. Called covenant marriage, the contract requires marital counseling prior to the wedding and, should it be necessary, before divorce proceedings. In addition, new techniques have rendered counseling a more effective tool in preserving marriages.

Violence Lessons. Claudia Dowling. *Mother Jones*, v. 23 pp32–41 July/August 1998.

Dowling writes that a history of family violence is one of the major forecasters of juvenile delinquency for children in later life. There are at least 3 million children living in abusive households in America, and researchers have discovered that children as young as two years old will imitate violent behaviors and may come to regard them as normal. Fifty percent of girls whose mothers are beaten will become involved with abusive men, and up to 75 percent of children who see their fathers beating their mothers have behavioral problems. The writer describes the case of Brenda Shores and her two children, Ernie and Brianna Cushman, and discusses the treatment the children have received at a summer camp program designed to help them express their worries and redirect their anger.

The Crime of Quality Time. Nathan Gardels. *New Perspectives Quarterly*, v. 15 pp25–31 1998.

In an interview, prominent social critic Christopher Lasch discusses the impact of America's liberal consumer culture on the family. He argues that the family has been reduced to its affectional core with the loss of all of its economic, educational, and authoritative functions. He contends that the predominance of child care in America is tending to produce the character traits, including bitterness, amorality, and aggression, of children raised without parents. Identifying the development of conscience as the real issue in this debate, he suggests that it requires both love and authority, and therefore also depends on the presence of the family. He concludes by observing that work will have to be differently organized to reconcile equality of employment with family life.

Mom vs. Mom. Ralph Gardner, Jr. *New York*, v. 35 pp20–25 October 21, 2002.

According to Gardner, working and nonworking mothers have become part of opposing camps. Those who have chosen to make a career of motherhood wonder whether they are missing out on a wonderful life, while many working mothers are concerned that they are sacrificing their families on the altar of their own ambition. Instead of directing their anger at corporate America's miserly, unpaid maternity leave and refusal to consider flextime, though, working and unworking mothers are venting their resentment and suspicion on each other.

Gay Families Come Out. Barbara Kantrowitz. *Newsweek*, v. 128 pp50–54+ November 4, 1996.

Kantrowitz says that same-sex parents are now attempting to come out of the shadows and into the mainstream. Being open does not guarantee acceptance, however. Many Americans remain very uncomfortable with the idea of gay parents because of their religious objections, genuine concern for the welfare of children, or bias against homosexuals in general. Congress recently passed a bill, which was signed by President Clinton, that allowed states to prohibit same-sex marriages. In addition, only 13 states specifically allow single lesbians or gay men to adopt, says the Lambda Legal Defense and Education Fund, a gay-rights advocacy group. Nonetheless, gays say that they hope being honest with the outside world will ultimately increase acceptance, just as parenthood makes them feel more related to their communities. The experiences of some gay parents and their children are presented.

Grandparents as Parents? Karen Miles. *Parenting*, v. 16 p214 September 2002.

As Miles reports, according to census figures, 3.8 million children in the United States are currently being raised by their grandparents. Drug and alcohol abuse by parents is one of the main reasons for this, but divorce, neglect, and mental health problems are also contributory factors, according to Sylvie de Toledo, director of Grandparents as Parents in Lakewood, California. Challenges grandparents face when they become second-time parents are discussed.

The Changing Face of Adoption. Kelly King Alexander. *Parents*, v. 76 pp134–140 September 2001.

Alexander says that an increasing number of couples with biological children are turning to adoption as a means of expanding their families. Similarly, adoptions by single people, same-sex couples, and "empty nesters" are on the increase. A 1997 survey by the National Center for Health Statistics discovered that for every domestic adoption, there are five or six would-be parents, nearly twice the number of a decade earlier. Ironically, this is happening at the same time that the total number of adoptions has actually fallen. The dizzying range of possibilities open to prospective adoptive parents gives them more choice, more voice, and more power, but it can also make the adoption process more daunting. The path can be cleared, however, by clarifying some common misconceptions and concerns. The writer explains how the adoption process works.

The Brady Bunch 2000. Holly Robinson. *Parents*, v. 75 pp147–154 November 2000.

Robinson writes that the reality of stepfamily life rarely lives up to expectations, in part because the concept of a wholly blended family is a myth. According to marriage, family, and stepfamily counselor Leslye Hunter, steprelationships can be loving and wonderful but are not the same as biological relationships, so each biological family remains separate within the new unit. No matter how strong the bond is between spouses, merging families is like living in a foreign country: It takes time to learn the customs and language and it is essential not to expect too much too soon. The challenges of making a new combined family work are discussed, and strategies to help combined families live together harmoniously are presented.

Midlife Moms. Karen S. Schneider. *People*, v. 57 pp80–86 April 29, 2002.

In a cover story, the writer discusses the joys and problems of late-life motherhood. In the last decade, the number of American mothers giving birth after 40 has almost doubled, to more than 94,000 in 2000. Celebrity mothers such as Geena Davis and Julianne Moore help draw attention to the possibilities of midlife motherhood, but a much-talked-about new book by economist Sylvia Ann Hewlett is raising important questions about the problems of getting pregnant after 40. In *Creating a Life: Professional Women and the Quest for Children*, Hewlett, who herself battled with late-life pregnancy, reminds readers that biology does not wait for any woman. She is supported by a Mayo Clinic study that argues that peak fertility occurs between 20 and 30 and then falls rapidly: 20 percent after 30, 50 percent after 35, and 95 percent after 40.

The American Family and the Nostalgia Trap. Stephanie Coontz. *Phi Delta Kappan*, v. 76 ppK1–K20 March 1995.

According to Coontz, it has become fashionable to blame a wide range of problems, including poverty, crime, drug abuse, unemployment, and social alienation, on the supposed breakdown of the family. Evidence from systematic research, however, suggests the opposite. Increasing rates of divorce and single parenthood are probably caused by rising unemployment, stagnant wages, decreased job security, and the breakdown of communities. The delinquent behavior attributed to children from broken homes is in fact more common among children from two-parent families in which the parents are in conflict or the father is disengaged. Stigmatizing single-parent families can make their difficulties worse. Instead, schools and other public agencies should recognize the potential strengths of families of all types and offer them the support they need.

The Fatherhood Industry. Judith Davidoff. *The Progressive*, v. 63 pp28–31 November 1999.

Established in 1994, the National Fatherhood Initiative is working to make responsible fatherhood a national priority, believing that fathers play a crucial role in the lives of children. Davidoff explains that, working in association with both the Governors' Task Force on Fatherhood Promotion and the bipartisan Congressional Task Force on Fatherhood Promotion, it is part of a nationwide movement focused on paternal duties. According to the National Center for Children in Poverty, all 50 American states have some type of responsible fatherhood program, ranging from public information campaigns to parenting classes for young fathers to job training for fathers in prison. The writer discusses the nature, extent, philosophy, and implications of the fatherhood promotion movement.

Prodding the Poor to the Altar. Barbara Ehrenreich. *The Progressive*, v. 65 pp14 15 August 2001.

Ehrenreich argues that conservatives are cooking up schemes to get poor women on welfare married off as quickly as possible. The idea of marrying off the welfare poor was embedded in the 1996 welfare reform law, which described marriage as the basis of a successful society and whose stated goals include ending dependency of needy parents on government benefits by promoting job preparation, work, and marriage and encouraging the formation and maintenance of two-parent families. To date, however, there has been no increase in weddings among single mothers in poverty, nor should marriage be expected to solve their problems. Recognizing that the chance to share a blue-collar male income is not, even for very poor women, a powerful attraction to marriage, the authorities are now pushing government-applied incentives to get people to marry. The writer explores the underlying motives of the conservative promarriage movement.

Divorced? Don't Even Think of Remarrying Until You Read This. Hara Estroff Marano. *Psychology Today*, v. 33 pp56–60, 62 March/April 2000.

Marano reports that an astounding 60 percent of remarriages fail after an average of ten years. The data reveal that when it comes to remarriage, previous experience is of little use: In fact, a previous marriage decreases the chances of a second marriage working. The writer discusses why people do not learn from the mistakes they made in their first marriage and why remarriage is so difficult.

The Marrying Kind. Tammerlin Drummond. *Time*, v. 157 p52 May 14, 2001.

According to Drummond, Vermont's civil-union law is making the state into the leading gay and lesbian honeymoon location. One year ago, Vermont became the first state in America to recognize same-sex civil unions—marriages in practically every legal respect except name—and 3,000 gays and lesbians have since come to the state to get married. Opponents' predictions that Vermont would become a "gay state" and that same-sex marriage would sweep the nation as homosexuals in other states demanded the same rights have not come true. Instead, the area is experiencing a small boom in gay tourism, with around 80 percent of the 2,000 gay civil-union licenses granted so far issued to out-of-state residents. Nationally, the battle over gay marriage continues, and over 30 states have passed "defense of marriage laws" that prevent same-sex unions from being recognized.

A Bad Start? Nadya Labi. *Time*, v. 153 p61 February 15, 1999.

Labi writes that, according to a controversial report, cohabiting may lead to divorce. Released by the National Marriage Project, the report also cites studies that found that couples who live together before getting married tended to have more incidents of domestic violence against women and physical and sexual abuse of children. Larry Bumpass, who is a sociologist at the University of Wisconsin, disputes the report, however, saying that the trend in divorce is over a hundred years old, which clearly means it was not caused by cohabitation.

American Families Are Drifting Apart. Barbara LeBey. *USA Today Magazine*, v. 130 pp20–22 September 2001.

LeBey explains that family estrangements are becoming more numerous, more profound, and more painful. The cracks in Americans' family structure became apparent in the mid-1970s when the divorce rate doubled; today, 51 percent of all marriages end in divorce. During the 1960s, the sexual revolution, the women's liberation movement, the states' relaxation of divorce laws, and the mobility of American families had a huge impact on the traditional family structure. These societal changes have converged to foster family alienation, exacerbate old family rifts, and create new ones. For the widely scattered baby boomers with more financial means than any generation before them, commitment, intimacy, and family togetherness have never been high on their list of priorities.

Interfaith Families Face "December Dilemma." *USA Today Magazine*, v. 125 pp4–5 December 1996.

Each December, the estimated 750,000 interfaith families in America face dilemmas relating to how to balance the celebrations of Christmas and Hanukkah. According to the writer, beneath these decisions runs a tension that can threaten to spoil what should be a joyful and renewing time of year.

Many interfaith couples are opting to celebrate both festivals; although this may make December an exhausting time, parents in interfaith families feel a deep sense of pride and achievement from having shared both Jewish and Christian celebrations with their children.

The Price of Child Abuse. Samantha Levine. *U.S. News & World Report*, v. 130 p58 April 9, 2001.

Levine reports on the hidden, lifelong costs attached to child abuse. Child abuse costs America upward of $94 billion every year, or $258 million a day. That is a $1,462 annual toll for every U.S. family, according to a first-of-its-kind study released recently by the Chicago-based group Prevent Child Abuse America. The report's estimated costs are calculated from various sources of information on everything from mental health care and juvenile justice to the costs of building and running adult prisons and even lost productivity in the workplace.

Wounding with Words. Rachel K. Sobel. *U.S. News & World Report*, v. 129 p53 August 28, 2000.

Sobel writes that a new study by sociologist Murray A. Straus says that too many parents lose control of their tempers when disciplining their children. A study of 991 parents has determined that virtually all Americans, regardless of their age, ethnicity, or socioeconomic classification, shout, scream, or use derogatory names in reference to their children, and in some instances the aggression is alarming. Straus warns that such occurrences can have serious reverberations. His earlier work has associated parental verbal aggression with kids' mental disorders, delinquency, depression, and bulimia.

Designer Babies. Shannon Brownlee. *The Washington Monthly*, v. 34 pp25–31 March 2002.

According to Brownlee, a huge, uncontrolled experiment in bioengineering humans is well under way in American fertility clinics. Today, any couple with several thousand dollars to spare can pick the sex of their offspring, and parents who are carriers for certain genetic disorders can undergo IVF and have the resulting embryos genetically tested to ensure their children do not have the disease. The fertility industry's efforts to assist couples in conceiving could one day bring society to the brink of altering the genetic heritage of the species. Thanks largely to abortion politics and Americans' collective squeamishness about intruding on the individual's right to become a parent, America has few mechanisms in place for controlling the pace of this technology, ensuring the safety of patients, or even talking about the ethics of such experiments.

Index